Santa Ana
MOUNTAINS
History, Habitat & Hikes

Santa Ana
MOUNTAINS
History, Habitat & Hikes

On the Slopes of Old Saddleback and Beyond

PATRICK MITCHELL

natural

HISTORY
PRESS

Published by Natural History Press
A Division of The History Press
Charleston, SC 29403
www.historypress.net

Front and back covers: San Mateo Canyon wilderness. *Photographs by the author.*
Back cover: Mariposa lilies. *Photograph by Joel Robinson.*

First published 2013

Manufactured in the United States

ISBN 978.1.60949.617.3

Library of Congress CIP data applied for.

I dedicate this book to my wonderful wife, Shannon, for pushing me to do what I love and standing by me when I fail. Her compassion, beauty and wisdom are as big as the mountains and as deep as the canyons. Without her support I could not have finished this book.

Contents

Preface

I grew up in the distant shadows of the Santa Ana Mountains in the hub of Orange County. I have been hiking in the range for nearly three decades. It was more than twenty-five years ago that this little mountain range began to earn my respect.

During an ecology field course in which we camped near the crest of the range, something was said that I found hard to believe but that also inspired me to explore the Santa Ana Mountains more fully. The instructor of the course was Richard Bates, and one evening after a campfire dinner, as we looked over the ridges and valleys of the western slope, he said, "You are looking at one of the wildest landscapes in Southern California. In fact," he explained, "the Santa Ana Mountains may be wilder than the Sierra Nevada." Mr. Bates, as we all came to know him, is a man full of knowledge and wisdom about wild and natural places. This statement proved no different.

It was hard to believe, but since that night on the ridge above Potrero Los Pinos and San Juan Capistrano, I have hiked nearly every trail and road that crosses the rugged slopes. I have read as many articles, books and scientific studies on the range and its inhabitants as I could find. I have even conducted my own research to benefit management of the San Mateo Canyon Wilderness Area. Several years before writing this rendition of a Santa Ana Mountains book, I even joined several others on an expedition of the range in which we filmed the month-long experience.

Before that, I worked for years as an activist trying to slow the development machine that was swallowing up the wild places where I learned to explore

There are many great views in the Santa Ana Mountains, like this one near Ladd Canyon.

but found that being on the losing side so often made it difficult to continue. I abandoned front-line activism to become an educator who shared the beauty of nature with people of all ages and backgrounds. In-your-face activism is for the young of heart and mind, and unfortunately, watching one-of-a-kind sacred solstice caves be blown from a hillside and seeing centuries-old oak trees crumble under the blade of a big yellow bulldozer made my heart old and filled my mind with too many sad memories. Today, I follow other great Western thinkers like Abbey and Foreman and let the young take conservation philosophies and run with them. My activism today consists of a one-on-one conversation, a letter to the editor or one to my local politician.

Sharing the good things in nature with people who were seeing them for the first time covers up the wounds and scars of activism—like a miracle cream available only in God's great mountains. Some of my favorite programs have taken place in the Santa Ana Mountains as I led inner-city teenagers on backpacking trips into the depths of San Mateo Canyon. One such trip with the Orange County Conservation Corps was a life-changing experience—for both the participants and for me.

I was at the head of a group of ten tough young men and women whose daily lives were harder and more complex than I wanted to ever experience. They talked tough, acted rough and were strong, with views on life that were very different from mine but still shaped from very real experiences. When the sun went down and bats and owls came out and coyotes howled, they became scared, lost and totally aware they were out of their element. And I was in mine. Several years after this trip, one of the young men contacted me. He wanted to know if I could write him a reference letter because he was applying for a job with California Fish and Game. He explained that the week in the wilderness changed his life. He said, "Now I know why you get so excited when you talk about nature." Little miracles like that make the wounds of battle heal quickly.

Through these experiences, I have found that although the peaks are not as high and the range is not as vast, the Santa Ana Mountains in many ways are at least as wild as the Sierra Nevada. But that is not all I have found. As development continues to chew up the foothills to the east and west of the range and new roads cut off corridors to the north and south, the ability of the mountains to maintain their wild heritage is diminished.

Many of the plants and animals in the range continue to be threatened by the loss of habitat. Large fires, new cities with roads and houses and other infrastructure replace the habitats and natural processes on which plants and animals have come to depend.

Another concern is that as the cities surrounding the Santa Anas continue to grow, more of the citizens who dwell there seek refuge from the urban environment by recreating in the wild canyons of this spectacular range. It is for these reasons that I wrote this book.

I hope that the information compiled herein will help keep the range wild, as well as help visitors to the Santa Anas feel like they have learned a little from the mountains. Although there are people out there who may know the range better than I do, and know better the parts and places, this book is probably the most complete and well-rounded body of information on the Santa Ana Mountains currently available. At least that has been the goal. So read on, and learn from these mountains as I have. Let them remain forever wild.

Acknowledgements

T his book would not have been possible without the love and support of my family. I love them back and thank them for sharing in the sacrifices of living with a naturalist and writer instead of a wealthy tycoon. I would like to thank Santa Ana College for providing field courses that introduce students to the natural lands of Southern California and for providing Richard Bates with a place to share his vast knowledge and experience. The writing of this book began as a senior project at Prescott College, where I learned that education is a journey, not a destination, and that science and spirituality are a powerful combination when rooted in the mind, heart and hands of a conservation naturalist.

This book has been a journey for sure. Thanks to Tom Fleischner and Walt Anderson for their inspiration and support at the onset of this project. I want to thank Jerry Roberts and The History Press, who found me at a time when I thought this book would never make it to press. I also want to thank Joel Robinson for his photos, encouragement and contributions to the Santa Ana Mountains. I would like to thank all the other naturalists, activists, settlers, rancheros and indigenous people who visited or lived in the Santa Ana Mountains before me. Their lives made this book possible.

Among the latter of these are Kirk Pickler and Chelsea Tran, who explored the range with me and Joel on the Santa Ana Mountains Ecosystem Expedition; the late Craig Benneville; and the rest of the OCEF! crew with whom I learned to stand up for this range while also taking the time to enjoy it. I am indebted to the Tongva and Acjachemen people who have shared their knowledge and history of the range with me. Their deep spiritual and ancestral connection to this place is something of which I can only dream. Thanks to Julie Lee and the Bowers Museum for making their historic images available and to Debra Clark and the Trabuco Ranger District for access to their archives and expertise. I would also like to thank the Heritage Museum of Orange County for access to their photos and maps. Finally, and most importantly, I thank God for making temples as glorious as the Santa Ana Mountains and for giving me the eyes, ears and mind to experience them.

Introduction

THIS BOOK AND ITS AUTHOR

From Long Beach to Oceanside and Fontana to Temecula, the Santa Ana Mountains are visible, standing as they have for twelve million years, keeping the desert from reaching the coast and now slowing civilization's march into the desert. Following is a brief introduction to a mountain range that is both socially important to the civilization that borders it and biologically important as an island of wilderness.

There are many sources of information on the Santa Ana Mountains, and they have all served me well in the compilation of this book. Some of those sources were researched and written by other naturalists and historians to whom I owe much gratitude. And I hope that this book honors their love of this mountain range as their work has helped me develop a passion for the canyons, ridges and slopes of these mountains. I have included a resource guide that will help readers connect to the range and to many of the authorities on the Santa Ana Mountains from whom I learned.

Although this book is not meant to be a field guide, it will serve readers while they are exploring the range. Stuff it in a backpack until you find a broad spreading oak on a ridge or deep in a canyon. Then sit down and, under the shade and shelter of that grand tree, pull it out and read about these mountains and the people, critters and events that preceded us here. And when you have taken in a story or two, stop, listen and watch—and that old oak you are sitting under will likely tell you a story of its own.

HUMANS AND THE SANTA ANA MOUNTAINS

The range is rich in human history, and historical landmarks abound. These landmarks include the home of the famous nineteenth-century actress Helena Modjeska, the locations of mining boomtowns and the spot of the capture and hanging of several bandits. At least a half dozen sites in the range are registered as California Historic Landmarks, and the number continues to grow.

Hundreds of Native American sites can be found in the Santa Ana Mountains. These sites range from bedrock mortars to ceremonial sites. Because of past vandalism and theft of artifacts, native people are hesitant to disclose the location of many sites. If you run across one of these special places, please leave everything as you found it and take nothing with you but memories.

Not all visitors to the mountains were as respectful as the native people who lived there. Hermits, bandits, murderers and ghosts have played a role in the rich history of the Santa Ana Mountains. It was, perhaps, Catholic-led Spanish Imperialists, though, who have had the greatest impact on the range and its peaks, canyons and creeks.

The first of the Spanish to visit the range was Gaspar de Portolà in 1769. He spent several days along the western slopes of the range, camping in Trabuco Canyon and just outside the range along Santiago Creek. His expedition is responsible for the naming of many natural features in the area.

Though the range is believed to have been first named by the Portolà Expedition, which camped at its base on Saint Anne's Day 1769, according to an 1801 map, the range we now know as the Santa Anas was divided into two ranges. The northern section was named the Sierra de Santiago, and the southern section was the Sierra de Trabuco. The highest peaks of the range, Santiago and Modjeska, seemed to be the dividing point. It was an 1860 map that first officially attributed the name Santa Ana to the range, calling the mountains the Sierra de Santa Ana. This map also appears to be the first official reference to "Old Saddleback," the name often given to the mountain and twin peaks of Santiago and Modjeska. Saddleback has also been known as Temescal Mountain and San Juan Mountain at various times and by different communities.

GEOGRAPHY, CLIMATE AND GEOLOGY

The Santa Ana Mountains are the westernmost range of the Peninsular Ranges, which also include the San Jacinto, Laguna and Santa Rosa Mountains. The Los Angeles Basin is included in the Peninsular Ranges as well. These ranges have a north–south crest with heavily eroded canyons to the west and east and are an extension of the Baja California Peninsula. The Peninsular Range Province once rested alongside mainland Mexico, but for the last twenty-five million years has been moving northward as a result of tectonic activity. The Santa Ana Mountains are separated from other mountain ranges by broad valleys but have managed to establish an extraordinary diversity of plants and animals, several of which are found nowhere else. Because of the relative geographic isolation and the spectacular representation of organisms, the Santa Ana Mountains provide both the amateur and the scientist an excellent opportunity for studying nature.

The range is outlined by natural as well as human features. The Santa Ana River, which has origins in all the major mountain ranges of Southern California and flows through San Bernardino and Riverside Counties, is the northern boundary and a corridor from which desert species have colonized the Santa Ana Mountains. Temescal, Elsinore and Temecula Valleys rest at the foot of the eastern escarpment of the range. Interstate 15 also follows the eastern escarpment and provides one of the most dramatic views of the range.

The Santa Margarita River, much of which is in Camp Pendleton Marine Corps Base, serves as the southern terminus of the range, at least as far as this work is concerned. (Some discrepancy exists among authorities and on many maps about what is actually the southern boundary of the range.) Many of the mountains rest within the base, and few members of the public ever get access to them. In other cases, the peaks and ridges have been given regional names that have caused some confusion among newcomers to the mountains. Geographically, and for simplicity, the Santa Margarita River is recognized by most as the southern terminus.

The western boundary of the range is often obscured by foothills, which in places stretch to the coast. For the purposes of this book, I have arbitrarily chosen Santiago and Limestone Canyons to the north and Bell Canyon to the south as the western boundary. Though it must be pointed out that history, both natural and cultural, is never so simplistic, and thus many stories and events cross these boundaries.

South of Ortega Highway (State Route 74), the western boundary is less definitive, and public access is limited, so no definite boundary has been set.

I assume, for personal convenience, that the boundary lies along an invisible line running southeast from Caspers Wilderness Park to Camp Pendleton.

The Santa Ana Mountains run parallel to the coast and are, on average, about twenty miles inland. On clear days, the Santa Anas command a view from almost anywhere in the Southland.

SIZE OF THE MOUNTAINS

At the longest points from north to south, the range measures about 62 kilometers, or 40 miles. At the widest point, the range is not more than 25 kilometers, or 18 miles. The total area of the Santa Ana Mountains, as far as this work is concerned, is about 1,150 square kilometers, or 720 square miles.

The peaks of Old Saddleback Mountain are more than a mile high. According to the United States Geologic Survey, Santiago Peak, the highest in the range, is 5,687 feet above sea level, and Modjeska Peak is 5,496 feet in elevation.

Three other peaks in the range are greater than 4,000 feet above sea level. Trabuco Peak is 4,604 feet, Los Pinos Peak is 4,510 feet and Pleasants Peak is 4,007 feet high. More than a half dozen of the lower peaks reach above 3,000 feet. The average elevation of the crest is above 1,000 meters, or 3,000 feet.

OWNERSHIP OF THE MOUNTAINS

Most of the range, or nearly 200,000 acres, is public land administered by the Trabuco Ranger District of the Cleveland National Forest and belongs to every American citizen. The federal government has maintained much of this land since 1893, when the Trabuco Canyon Forest Reserve was established. It became the Trabuco National Forest in 1906 but was enlarged and added to the Cleveland National Forest two years later. The remaining land is in Orange, Riverside and San Diego Counties and is mostly private property.

The Cleveland National Forest has set aside nearly forty thousand acres as wilderness, and thousands of acres have been set aside in private reserves and regional parks, including the Irvine Ranch Conservancy, a National

Natural Scenic Landmark; the Santa Rosa Plateau Ecological Preserve; and the Wildlands Conservancy's Mariposa Preserve.

Unfortunately, these set-asides are merely a fraction of the range and are too widely scattered to provide adequate protection for all the historic resources and plants and animals that call the Santa Anas home. This is especially true as development creeps farther into the foothills of the range, shrinking the usable habitat and creating fragments of an ecosystem. As these habitat fragments become isolated, the wildlife populations in them become doomed.

ACCESS TO THE MOUNTAINS

Access to the range is fairly easy, with several freeways surrounding the range and a state highway crossing it. Ortega Highway (California 74), a state-designated scenic route, is the easiest route to major recreational points within the mountains. From Interstate 5 on the west side and I-15 on the east, Ortega Highway can be taken to the San Mateo Canyon Wilderness Area, Caspers Regional Park and Forest Service Campgrounds.

Interstate 15 and California Highway 91, both of which lead into the city of Corona, provide access to the northern sections of the range. From downtown Corona, take Lincoln Avenue south to Chase Drive and go west to Skyline Drive, which leads into the mountains. Indian Truck Trail, Clinton Keith Road and De Luz Road are accessible from Interstate 15 and lead to southeastern portions of the range and to San Mateo Canyon Wilderness Area.

The western slope has the most convenient points of access. Santiago Canyon Road (S18), which can be reached by heading east on Chapman Avenue from the 55 Freeway, connects with roads leading to most of the major canyons on the west side. Black Star Canyon, Silverado Canyon, Modjeska/Harding Canyons and Trabuco Canyon can all be reached from Santiago Canyon Road. Ken Croker's *Santa Ana Mountains Trailguide* has accurate directions to more than thirty-five trails in the range but has been out of print for many years and may be hard to find. Franko's Maps also makes a thorough Santa Ana Mountains trail map. Both these resources are recommended for those who wish to further explore the mountains.

Preparations for the Mountains

Before going to the Santa Ana Mountains, be aware of the dangers that lurk there, and take proper steps to avoid any unexpected hardships. The primary dangers of the range are heat, rugged terrain, rattlesnakes, mountain lions, ticks and poison oak. Being able to identify these is the first step to avoiding any unwanted difficulty. I have had my fair share of run-ins with each of these and cannot stress enough how important this preparation is.

To avoid problems associated with rugged terrain, stay on trails and roads and use topographic maps whenever possible. Today's reliance on GPS technology is no substitute for good planning and a keen sense of place. Rattlesnakes are not regularly encountered, but one should always keep an open ear for their unmistakable warning. I have encountered only a couple dozen "buzzworms" in the last ten years of extensive exploration in the range, and none has presented any danger other than a brief delay in travel time. Cross-country travel offers a more likely rattlesnake encounter than trails and roads do. Remember that the snake's rattle is a warning. He knows you are too big to eat and that you are more dangerous to him than he is to you. Heed the warning!

The chance of running across a mountain lion, and knowing it, is not very likely; however, if it does happen, the best thing to do is make a lot of noise and stand as tall as possible. The bigger you look, the safer you will be. If small children are present, pick them up and hold on to them; kids and adults have been attacked by lions in the Santa Ana Mountains. Because of their size, children resemble natural prey. Never turn your back on a mountain lion, and do not run.

I had never had a problem with ticks, but a few years ago I took my oldest son on a hike in Limestone Canyon, and he came back with several behind his ears and around his neck. Needless to say, my wife was not pleased, and I have paid close attention ever since. If one is encountered, save it after removal and show it to a doctor as a precaution for Lyme disease, though it is not a problem in our region. Place the tick in a zip-lock bag and stash it away in case of sickness.

There are numerous methods of tick removal. I usually heat the end of a pair of tweezers and waive it near the tick before using it to pull out the little critters. The heat seems to encourage the ticks to release their hold and to come out easily.

Knowing how to identify poison oak in all its growth forms and in all seasons is the best defense against being infected by it. All canyons in the range are thick with poison oak, especially in wet years.

There is very little water in the Santa Anas during dry seasons and years. Water may be found in creeks during winter and spring but must be treated before drinking. Springs and canyon pools exist much of the year but should not be counted on and should also be treated before drinking. Always bring plenty of water with you wherever you travel in the backcountry. I wouldn't dream of entering the range for a hike with anything less than a quart, and I usually bring my water pump with me.

Following is a list of things I pack when going to the Santa Ana Mountains.

Water (minimum of 1 quart)
First aid supplies, including snake bite kit (know how to use it)
Hat
Sunglasses
Sunscreen
Windbreaker or rain jacket
Maps
Compass
Binoculars
Flashlight
Trail guide
Field guides

As one's experience in the range increases, additions and subtractions to the list may be warranted. For overnight trips in the range, see one of the many guides to backpacking for a pack list.

CLIMATE OF THE MOUNTAINS

Southern California has a near-perfect climate, and as part of Southern California, the Santa Ana Mountains are no exception. Climate is the historical record of temperature, precipitation, air pressure and movement—collectively, weather.

Several factors work together to determine a region's climate. These are latitude, topography and distance from the ocean. The Santa Ana Mountains are between thirty-three and thirty-four degrees latitude, a zone often associated with deserts. The Santa Ana Mountains are located approximately twenty miles from the Pacific Ocean and are the only significant relief between the coast and the higher San Jacinto Mountains to the east. A combination of maritime and Mediterranean climates are at work in the Santa Ana Mountains.

Most weather affecting the Santa Ana Mountains comes from the Pacific Ocean, including rain, snow and fog. Because of their proximity to the coast and their three-thousand-foot crest, the Santa Ana Mountains are a major obstacle preventing many weather systems from reaching the Elsinore and Temecula Valleys east of the range. The Peninsular Ranges, of which the Santa Anas are part, cast a rain shadow over the deserts of Southern California, stealing most of the moisture released from clouds as they attempt to rise over the peaks and ridges.

Contrary to popular belief, Southern California does have four seasons. The changes are not always as obvious as they might be in the Midwest or Northeast, but for the explorer in the Santa Ana Mountains, there are signs to look for.

Winter is the wet season in the range. Average annual precipitation in the Santa Anas is almost thirty-four inches, although that varies with elevation. Winter is also the growing season, as much of the vegetation goes dormant during the summer droughts. The hills and grasslands, reacting to the rain, turn from golden brown and amber to sparkling emerald green.

Unlike in regions farther north, rainstorms and cloudy conditions are not an everyday occurrence during winter in the Santa Anas. In fact, many winter days are cloudless and warm, allowing distant views of the snow-covered peaks of the San Gabriel, San Jacinto and San Bernardino Mountains. Average January temperatures range from forty-four to fifty-two degrees and, like precipitation, depend greatly on elevation.

When it does rain, it often pours, and flooding results in many of the canyons, washing out bridges and roads. Landslides occur here as well. During the extremely wet winter of 1992–93, many homes in the foothills and lower elevations were damaged as the slopes on which they were built gave way, causing millions of dollars' worth of damage and destroying many homes.

Winter precipitation is mostly in the form of rain, although some snow falls on the higher peaks, mostly above four thousand feet. Snow doesn't last very long, usually melting after a few days. On rare occasions, the snowfall is significant, and I have heard of folks cross-country skiing the Main Divide Truck Trail, which follows the crest of the range.

Spring brings flowers and fog to the Santa Ana Mountains. If winter rains have been significant, flowers will bloom from March into August, with the peak in May. Fogs continue through September.

The California Current, which brings cold water from the Arctic to the coast of California, is the source of Southern California's morning fogs, known regionally as the marine layer. This fog is trapped in the Los Angeles Basin by the mountains that surround it. Fog is responsible for a small amount of the measured precipitation in the Santa Anas and may be the reason certain plants in the range survive summer droughts. The flora of the range is spectacular, and spring is the time to see it. Spring is also the ideal time to hike in the Santa Anas, with average temperatures in the sixty-five-degree range.

By June, the hills have begun their retreat back to gold and amber, and the summer dormancy period has begun. Some fog still reaches the Santa Anas in summer but is burned away early in the day, revealing the haze and smog for which Los Angeles is famous. Occasionally, small remnants of tropical storms from the Gulf of Mexico will move northwest and reach Southern California, but more often than not, only the highest elevations get rain from them. Summer in the Santa Anas is not only dry but also hot. Average July temperatures are between sixty-eight and eighty-five degrees, although mid-day temperatures of ninety degrees or more are not uncommon.

Summer is the beginning of the windy season in Southern California. Cold air that makes it past the mountains is quickly consumed by the deserts. Occasionally, high pressure cells build up in the desert, forcing air back toward the coast. As the air drops back into the Los Angeles Basin through the Santa Ana River Valley, it is heated by compression. These strong winds, known as the Santa Ana Winds, are perhaps the best relief to the smog that lingers in the basin through summer and fall.

The Santa Ana Winds are hot and dry and become uncomfortable quickly. They also help spread fires, making the firefighter's job difficult and dangerous. Autumn is fire season in the Santa Ana Mountains, with a major fire every decade or so. The fires in the fall of 1993, and again in 2007 and 2008, proved this when thirty thousand acres burned all three years in the Santa Ana Mountains. Smaller fires occur every year. The temperature remains hot through fall, with little or no precipitation to relieve parched vegetation. Sunny, dry conditions are the rule, not the exception, and this continues into November. Fall is the worst time to visit the slopes of the Santa Anas, although comfortable conditions often still exist in the canyons of the range.

The topography of the Santa Ana Mountains has an outstanding effect on weather in Southern California. Localized inversion layers and differences in precipitation are evidence of this.

A rare scene of snow-covered peaks is captured south of Old Saddleback.

An inversion layer is formed when air heats as it rises, forming a lid over cold surface air. The Santa Ana Mountains are an eastern wall for the Los Angeles Basin inversion, holding in coastal fog and haze. The inversion layer is about 3,500 feet above sea level, very close to the elevation of the Santa Ana Mountains' crest.

During winter, storms coming off the ocean release precipitation as they are forced up and over the Santa Anas. Higher elevations receive the most rain, and areas east of the range, in the rain shadow, receive the least. Major storm systems cross the Santa Anas with little problem, but smaller localized systems drain themselves while crossing the range, leaving little moisture for the arid valleys to the east.

The average annual rainfall from 1985 to 1992 further supports this. Santiago Peak, at 5,687 feet, averaged 30.56 inches annually, while Silverado Canyon, at about 1,800 feet, averaged 16.24 inches; the city of Santa Ana, at an elevation of less than 200 feet, averages 13.00 inches annually.

Whatever the season or current weather, the Santa Ana Mountains provide the nearby human population with a great escape from the doldrums of modern civilization, while at the same time serving as a home for thousands of plants and animals. I encourage readers to explore the Santa Anas in all seasons, as each one holds unique treasures to discover.

GEOLOGY OF THE MOUNTAINS

The Santa Ana Mountains are part of the geographic province known as the Peninsular Ranges. The Peninsular Ranges make up most of Southern California west of, and including, the San Jacinto and Santa Rosa Mountains and also include the Los Angeles Basin and Channel Islands. Approximately twenty-five million years ago, the Peninsular Ranges were part of mainland Mexico and have been moving northward along the San Andreas Fault, probably since that time. All of the mountains in this province are fault-block mountains.

The range, at a glance, resembles the Sierra Nevada in shape, if not size, and is, in places, equally as rugged. The eastern escarpment of the range is almost vertical, while the western slope tilts gently toward the ocean. Deep, narrow canyons rest between peaks and plateaus and are continuously cut by perennial streams. The major drainages of the range include Santiago Creek, a tributary of the Santa Ana River; Trabuco Creek; Aliso Creek; San Juan Creek; and San Mateo Creek—all flowing west into the Pacific Ocean. Easterly flowing streams include Leech, McVicker, Horsethief, Mayhew, Coldwater, Bedford, Hagador and Tin Mine Creeks. All of these except Leech Creek, which flows directly into Lake Elsinore, feed Temescal Creek, a tributary to the Santa Ana River. These drainage systems once fed extensive marshes and wetlands on the way to the ocean but have, over the last five decades, been filled or channelized for "flood control" purposes. Only in the Santa Ana Mountains do these creeks still represent wild, dynamic systems. The Santa Margarita River at the southern edge of the range is a Wild and Scenic–candidate river that runs unobstructed for nearly all of its length.

Geologically speaking, the Santa Ana Mountains are a young mountain range, and because of this, they are especially rugged, as erosion hasn't yet had time to soften all the edges. To be round is every rock's desire, regardless of its size or location. What relief is apparent in the range can be attributed to differential erosion and displacement. The range has high seismic activity but no current volcanic potential. Folding is also locally significant in the Santa Anas.

Soil in the range is generally fairly shallow, with bedrock usually less than twenty feet below the surface. No significant agriculture takes place in the range, except for livestock grazing and the occasional illegal crop of cannabis.

Landslides are common in the Santa Ana Mountains, especially along roads, trails and other developments. Recent wet winters have caused extensive slippage and forced entire hillside neighborhoods to be evacuated, costing homeowners and cities millions of dollars.

The Santa Ana Mountains first began to appear more than twelve million years ago. Like all of the mountains in the Peninsular Ranges, the Santa Ana Mountains were uplifted due to activity along a fault. The Elsinore Whittier Fault is responsible for lifting the Santa Ana Mountains and is the reason for the Elsinore, Murrieta and Glen Ivy Hot Springs. The San Juan Hot Springs are the result of a smaller, inactive fault within the range. Prado Dam, which holds back the Santa Ana River on the northern boundary of the range, is built directly on top of the Elsinore Fault. It's no surprise that most of the residents along the Santa Ana River are required to have flood insurance.

Prior to the uplift of the Santa Ana Mountains, a shallow sea covered the area, depositing sediments we now find as limestone, siltstone and sandstone. Evidence in the sedimentary rock layers of the range suggests that since uplifting began, the range has been invaded by seas at least five times. During the Cretaceous period, the range was merely coastal hills and islands surrounded by a shallow sea.

Samples of nearly every rock type can be found in the Santa Anas, and a diversity of minerals has been located and extracted from the range. Clay, quartz and calcite are the most common minerals. Building and decorative stones are quarried in the range, including sand, gravel, roofing material, clay and concrete. Some marble has been extracted also.

According to a 1973 California Division of Mines and Minerals map, claims have been staked in the range for uranium/thorium 151, gold, copper, tin, lead, silver, zinc, coal, gypsum, sand, clay and gravel. Few of these have been commercially successful, with clay, sand and gravel being the commercial standouts.

Silverado Canyon experienced a silver mining boom at one time; however, it was short lived. Both sides of the range have had mines claiming to extract tin. Coal was mined in the Santa Anas. Records from the Mission San Juan Capistrano suggest that local natives mined for placer gold in Lucas Canyon, but this seems to have been of only limited economic value. A more detailed discussion of the area's mining history can be found in Part I.

Igneous Rocks

Geologists have decided that all rocks fit into three categories based on how they were formed. Igneous rocks, those that formed from molten material, are further divided into two types. Intrusive igneous rocks are those that formed beneath the surface of the earth—like granite, for example.

The granitic rock found in the Santa Ana Mountains is part of the Southern California Batholith (*bathos*=deep; *lithos*=rock). The Southern California Batholith consists of two separate intrusive units: gabbro and granite. The gabbro is dark in color, and the granite is lighter, but their textures are similar. The rock that makes up the Southern California Batholith is one hundred to ninety million years old. The batholith is exposed in the southern part of the range. The Morgan Trail into San Mateo Canyon Wilderness is an excellent place to see these rock types. For those who don't want to pound a trail, the summit of Ortega Highway passes near a few outcrops of the batholith.

The second type of igneous rock is extrusive igneous, or those rocks that hardened on the surface of the earth, and most are volcanic in origin. At least two volcanic events are represented in the Santa Ana Mountains. Island-arc volcanics from the Mesozoic era, 245 to 66 million years ago, are represented on several peaks, including Santiago Peak. More than 50 million years later, during the Miocene epoch (Cenozoic era), several eruptions of a now-vanished volcano left us with the El Modeno Volcanics.

These Batholithic rocks are located off the Morgan Trail.

The El Modeno Volcanics are named for the nearby community of El Modena, but an early geologist apparently misspelled the name and it was never corrected. Remnants of the historic volcano can still be found below the Orange Hill Restaurant and above the Orange County Mining Company Restaurant.

Metamorphic Rocks

The second category of rock we will discuss is metamorphic rocks. These are rocks whose structures have been significantly altered over time by heat and pressure. Metamorphic rocks are probably the least seen in the Santa Ana Mountains, although the majority of the range is probably made up of such rocks. In fact, the core (Bedford Canyon Formation) of the Santa Ana Mountains is metamorphic or partly metamorphosed rock that, prior to changing, was sedimentary in structure.

Metamorphic rock can be found at the edge of batholithic outcrops. These are older than nearby members of the Southern California Batholith and include schists, quartzites and marbles. Small exposures of metamorphic rock are visible at road cuts along middle sections of Ortega Highway. The Bedford Canyon Formation, formed during the late Jurassic period, is metamorphosed siltstone and can be found in many of the canyons on the west side, including Silverado and Modjeska Canyons, and of course in Bedford Canyon on the east side.

Sedimentary Rocks

Perhaps the most commonly seen rocks in the Santa Ana Mountains are sedimentary rocks. These are layers of sediments that were laid down by shallow seas, streams or wind and are cemented together over time to form rock. Geologists further divide this category into sedimentary environments, giving us Continental, Shoreline and Marine sedimentary rocks. For purposes of this book, Continental and Shoreline layers will be referred to generally as terrestrial sediments.

Marine sediments are common in the Santa Ana Mountains and have produced an abundance of fossils. Seas have covered this area no fewer than six times over the last 245 million years, and the rocks that resulted have taught us a great deal about the area's environment at those times. Fossils are more fully discussed later in this section.

One of the most interesting of the marine sedimentary layers is exposed near the joining of Silverado Creek with Santiago Creek. Numerous fossils have been collected here, including the only dinosaur bones ever found in Orange County, and a number of ammonites, a few of which were longer than a meter. This layer of shale dates back approximately 80 million years to the Cretaceous period and is known as Holtz Shale. Farther up Silverado Canyon, this layer meets up with the Baker Canyon Conglomerates, of similar age and which are also fossiliferous.

The Vaqueros Formation, formed from sediments deposited by a shallow sea during the Oligocene to early Miocene epochs, is a coarse sand and gravel formation also rich in fossils. The Vaqueros and Sespe (discussed below) Formations are so closely aligned in the Santa Ana Mountains that they are treated as a single formation, despite very different means of formation.

Marine layers from the Miocene epoch are represented by the yellow Topanga sandstone laid down between five million and twenty-five million years ago. This rock can be seen along Santiago Canyon Road and in the lower reaches of Silverado Canyon. Strong wind over millions of years has cut grottoes and holes into this layer. Legend holds that bandits utilized these caves between raids on the nearby town of Santa Ana during the 1800s. Native people also made use of these caves, as evidenced by the numerous artifacts that have been recovered from them.

Marine limestones are common throughout the Santa Anas and are easy to locate by finding one of the many cement plants that operate in the range. Limestone Canyon and Lucas Canyon are both excellent places to view limestone outcrops, which make up portions of the larger marine formations.

Due to the many advances and retreats of seas over this area, numerous marine layers have been laid down. They are exposed throughout the range. I have included cross sections from various canyons in the range to give a more complete view of the sedimentary picture. Highway 74 crosses several marine formations from the Mesozoic and Cenozoic eras and provides an excellent way to see much of the geologic record preserved in the Santa Ana Mountains.

The Santa Ana Mountains also contain numerous layers of the terrestrial-based sediments. The Bedford Canyon Formation is the oldest terrestrial formation in the range, dating back 210 million years to the early Jurassic or late Triassic periods. Rocks of this formation are partly metamorphosed.

Some fifty million years later, the Trabuco Conglomerate was deposited. Conglomerates are coarse, rounded gravels greater than two millimeters in

These red rocks are located near the mouth of Black Star Canyon.

diameter that have been cemented together. This reddish layer is apparent in many of the canyons on the northern part of the range, including Black Star, Modjeska and Trabuco Canyons.

During the Cenozoic era, several more layers were laid down. During the Eocene era, forty million years ago, the Sespe Formation, a continental-based sedimentary layer, was deposited in a marsh-like environment in between the retreat and advance of seas in the area. The resulting red siltstone is exposed in Black Star Canyon.

Where the Sespe Formation meets the Vaqueros Formation west of Santiago Road, one of the area's greatest geologic wonders can be found. "The Sinks," also known as Orange County's "Grand Canyon," is an area of landslides and badlands that have formed over centuries to create numerous pinnacles, basins and canyons resembling more a scene from the Four Corners region than one from Orange County. This area has been set aside, at least for now, as an open space reserve. The area is now protected as part of the Irvine Ranch Conservancy.

Fossils

When most people think of fossils, they think of the large dinosaur skeletons found at natural history museums. Other than a few marine mammals and some prehistoric cats, horses and camels, no large complete skeletons have been found in the range.

Following are the descriptions of some of the most common fossils found in the range.

Turritella fossils are perhaps the most common in the range, with at least six species and several variations having been recovered here. The conical shells belonged to snails that inhabited fairly shallow seas from the Cretaceous to recent times. The shells are usually whorled with raised or indented ribs.

Cucullaea make up two species of clams whose fossils can be found in the Santa Ana Mountains. The fossils range in size from less than one inch to more than three inches across. Both species have winged shells.

Chlamys are clams from the Miocene and Pliocene epochs. They have broad, prominent ribs radiating from folds of shells. These clams range in size from an inch or less to six or more inches across.

The *Hadrosaur* is a duck-billed dinosaur that lived near the shore of an ancient sea during the Late Cretaceous period. Only two Hadrosaur fossils have ever been found in the range. A fragment of jaw bone with two teeth in it was found near Santiago Canyon in 1933, and an ankle bone was found in the same area in the early 1990s. According to Carol Stadum in her book *A Student's Guide to Orange County Fossils*, some saurian bones have been collected on the eastern escarpment of the range near Corona.

Shark teeth and *bat ray* tooth plates are found in the range, as are ancient fish and bird bones. Other animal fossils found in the area, but not necessarily in the Santa Ana Mountains as defined in this book, include *turtles, horses, rhinoceroses, camels, sloths* and *mammoths*. Fossilized wood and vegetation can also be found in the Santa Ana Mountains. Ancient marshes and lagoons that once rested in the area of the Santa Anas have produced low-grade coal as well as fossils. A large *fossilized tree*, recovered near Irvine Lake, can be found on display at Chapman University.

Now that you know a little about the range, go there and see it for yourself. The following parts in this book will help you understand the cultural history and the flora and fauna of the Sierra de Santa Ana while you're there.

PART I

Cultural History

The deep canyons and rugged ridges of the Santa Ana Mountains hold a thousand stories of Southern California's rich human history. The cultures and the people have changed, as has their relationship with the land, but every era, nonetheless, has left its influence on the range.

Ghosts, bandits, mountain men and native people all have shaped the volumes of human history that surround the Sierra de Santa Ana. The following sections will tell the stories of a few of these people and the cultures that led them to, or kept them in, the Santa Ana Mountains.

THE FIRST PEOPLE

When the first European stood on the coastal plain of what is now Orange County and peered east up the slopes of Old Saddleback, nearly ten thousand indigenous people lived in the Los Angeles Basin. Perhaps another ten thousand people inhabited the arid lands immediately east of the Santa Ana Mountains. All of these people were members of six tribes.

Four of the six tribal groups lived in or utilized the Santa Ana Mountains, and all traded amongst one another and with other, more distant tribes. All of the indigenous cultures that called the Santa Anas home spoke languages that are of Shoshonean or Uto Aztecan origin. The Hopi, Comanche and Piute tribes speak languages similar to the Southern California groups, and even the famous female tracker and guide Sacagawea spoke a Uto Aztecan dialect. The languages associated with our local tribal groups extended all the way into central and southern Mexico.

The Shoshonean tribes, however, were not the first to come to the Santa Anas. People have been in and around California for nearly fifteen thousand years. The Folsom Clovis, or Early Man, culture is known to have come into California around 12,000 BC. Some archaeological records suggest that there may have been people here (Calico Hills) much earlier than that.

We can be quite confident that the Santa Ana Mountains region has been continuously inhabited for at least nine thousand years and possibly as long as eleven thousand years. The first inhabitants of the region were likely nomadic and followed game for subsistence. There are those who theorize that these early inhabitants hunted horse, camel and even bison in California and drove these large animals to extinction. The archaeological and fossil records tell us that these animals were, in fact, present at the same time as the earliest human inhabitants. The exact reason for the extinction of these animals is, however, speculation. We do know that as the Ice Age ended, people were hunting and gathering along the ocean shores of what is now Orange County.

Sometime between five and seven thousand years ago, these nomadic people began to settle and create more permanent dwelling sites. Grinding stones for turning seeds into flour began to appear around this time, and tools became more specialized during this period.

The people of Southern California lived peacefully with one another, enjoying relative harmony broken up by only the occasional and inevitable family squabble. This peaceful coexistence continued until 1769, when Europeans made contact with the first peoples of the region. At that time, the four tribal groups living in, or utilizing lands within, the Santa Ana Mountains were the Tongva/Gabrielino, the Ajachamen/Juaneño, Payomkowishum/Luiseno and the Taaqtam/Serrano.

These tribal groups are often best known by their given names, which, in most cases, are associated with the missions where they were forced to relocate as a labor force. For instance, the Gabrielino were moved to Mission San Gabriel, the Juaneño to the Mission San Juan Capistrano and the Luiseno to Mission San Luis Rey. The *Serranos* name comes from the Spanish and means "mountain dwellers" or "highlanders."

To honor these people and their cultures, we will use the traditional tribal names as much as is feasible. For the sake of clarity and better understanding, both traditional and given names will be used together, at least in the beginning of this account.

The northern Santa Ana Mountains are recognized as the territory of the Tongva/Gabielino people, who occupied much of the Los Angeles Basin. According to A.L. Kroeber, the Tongva lands in the Santa Ana Mountains stretched south from the range's northern boundary to Santiago Peak and Aliso Creek as it flowed west toward the ocean. The crest of the range was the eastern boundary of Gabrielino territory and the western boundary of Luiseno territory.

The Luiseno claim the central and southeastern escarpment of the range to its southern terminus and all the way to the coast from San Onofre Creek southward, well beyond the Santa Ana Mountains. Luiseno territory also extended eastward some distance to the boundaries of the Cahilla peoples' territory.

The northeastern portion of the range from Coldwater Canyon north to the Santa Ana River was also shared by the Taaqtam/Serrano people, who seasonally moved in and out of most of the mountains of Southern California. The Serrano were likely the most nomadic of the tribal groups in Southern California.

Tucked between the Gabrielino and the Luiseno west of the Santa Ana crest from Aliso Creek south to San Onofre Creek was Ajachemen/ Juaneño territory.

Neither the Gabrielino nor the Juaneño have been recognized by the U.S. government as sovereign tribal nations. At the time of this writing, both tribes have petitions before the Bureau of Indian Affairs for recognition.

Elders from all of these tribes have expressed to me that the boundaries discussed above were soft lines made hard only by European-based imperialistic necessity. Prior to the late 1700s, the lands within the Santa Ana Mountains were shared, and all the tribes considered themselves stewards of the resources found there.

The four tribes shared similar customs and traditions and communicated with one another, although their dialects differed slightly. Warfare between and among the tribes seems to have been almost nonexistent. The groups lived as large clans in permanent and semipermanent villages.

Trading routes were established over the Santa Ana Mountains, allowing coastal people to trade with the people of the deserts. Many of the ancient routes used by native people are still maintained by the U.S. Forest Service today as recreational trails and truck roads.

The tribal groups of the Santa Ana Mountains, along with their northern neighbors, the Chumash, were considered to be advanced cultures. Each tribe observed detailed ceremonies and religious practices, including the jimson weed (sacred datura) rituals. The tribes or nations maintained a hierarchical governing structure within clans and even today maintain tribal councils and democratic procedures.

Most of the indigenous people in and around the Santa Ana Mountains made homes of thatched reeds or other material placed on a framework of willow poles. These homes were called *kitches*. Size and shape of these dome-like structures may have varied from place to place, as very little has been recorded about them. It is likely that each structure housed a family unit, and thus the homes were built to suit the size of each family.

Cattails were most often used as the covering of these structures; the long, flat leaves or blades made excellent "shingles," carrying the occasional rainfall or dew off the structure. The three-foot-long cattail blades were cut and dried. Once they were brown but still maintained some flexibility, the leaf blades were tied into bundles three to six inches wide. Then, starting at the bottom of the frame, the bundles would be tied to the lateral sections of the willow frame. This process continued working around and then up the structure until it was completely covered. The bundles were tied tightly together to prevent drafts or water from entering the structure.

Unlike the Juaneño and Gabrielino, the Luiseno, who inhabited the southern end of the range, made permanent earth-covered houses. These structures resembled Navajo *hogans* from the Four Corners region of the southwestern United States.

The indigenous tribes who lived in and around the Santa Ana Mountains are an artistic people. Their basketry is among the finest known worldwide. The use of deer grass, basket rush, willow and other native plants allowed for elite weavers to make baskets so tight they could hold water and so strong they could hold a person. The fibers were dyed using California walnut, wild grapes, alder and other pigments ground and squeezed from local resources and allowing for intricate designs full of meaning and significance to the weavers and eventual owners of the baskets. Every basket was woven for a specific purpose. Some were granaries; some were flat and broad, used for separating chaff from seed; and still others carried babies and infants.

Many of the baskets made by the Southern California Indians are prized by collectors and museums. Bowers Museum in Santa Ana has a wonderful collection of old baskets. In addition, the basket-weaving tradition continues, and many local indigenous women continue to weave and sell their baskets today.

Families and clans returned year after year to the same stands of plants to harvest basket-making materials. They tended these "gardens" by harvesting

This meadow below El Cariso Village is known as Acjachemen Meadow. It's been known as a popular gathering place for indigenous basket-making materials.

just the right level of seed or stalk and making sure to remove weeds that might invade or overtake their prized plants. In some cases, small fires would be set to burn off undesirable species or encourage growth of the desirable ones. One such place is believed to be Acjachemen Meadow, a small *potrero* off Ortega Highway just west of El Cariso Village. This meadow is clearly visible on the south side of the road. In fall, native women and their families can be seen gathering from this place just as they have for hundreds of years.

Many animal effigies carved from soapstone have been discovered in and around the Santa Ana Mountains. The soft, pliable stone was abundant in large sedimentary veins on Santa Catalina Island, where island clans would have traded with mainland clans for large mammal skins, obsidian and other resources that were scarce on the island but regularly available on the mainland. The effigies were usually animal forms or representations and were likely ceremonial in nature. A few archaeologists have surmised that the small statues may have been traded and held for economic value also.

Pottery is known on the west side only from post-mission times; however, there is some evidence that the rich red clay deposits on the east side were utilized by the native people before European contact. In any case, the natives and later rancheros found immediate use for the high-quality clay found near Elsinore and Temescal.

Sand paintings associated with various rituals are known from all the tribes inhabiting the Santa Ana Mountains. As ceremony, colored sands would be used to "paint" representations of wishes or prayers at sacred locations and left for the wind. It was believed that as the wind blew the sand away, the prayers were carried to the spirits. Although I have never created a sand painting, I have often found what I believed to be sacred places in the range, and I have left many a prayer there hoping the wind would carry it to the hands of God.

Rock art in the form of petroglyphs and pictographs can be found in and immediately around the Santa Ana Mountains. These often-colorful murals served as history books for the tribes and clans that used these areas. Photos of some of this art are included here, but the locations of these sites must

remain secret as the level of vandalism and theft has made publicizing these important sites a recipe for their destruction. If you find one of these sites, please remember that they tell the story of one's ancestors and must be treated with the most respect.

How developed or defined was the culture of Santa Ana Mountain tribes? One of the ways social groups are judged is by their religious practices, and all of the tribal groups using the Santa Ana Mountains had many. In fact, most of the tribal groups followed some form of deep, meaningful worship. The most powerful of the gods inducing fear and providing blessings was Chiningchinich. The Acjachemen/Juaneño

We can only guess about the meaning of this rock art from the range, but we can be sure it had great meaning to its author.

oral history tells that this super being dwells in the heart of Old Saddleback. The Acjachemen believe that good acorn years, wet winters and abundant game all are in the hands of Chiningchinich. Likewise, firestorms, droughts and grizzly bears all were delivered to the people by Chiningchinich for their misdeeds or weak faith.

Rituals for all the tribes generally were of two types: a coming-of-age ceremony for boys and girls and, of course, the funeral-like mourning ceremonies. All of the tribal groups carried out some sort of jimson weed rituals in which a spirit animal guide would be adopted, visualized and learned from. Tests of one's strength and endurance usually followed the jimson weed ceremony. Participants would be laid on an ant hill and whipped with nettles. This was considered an important part of the puberty rites. Those who failed were considered weak and were pitied by other tribal members.

The "yoba" was a roofless circular structure constructed similarly to the kitche homes. This structure was likely a sort of community room used for spiritual ceremonies.

These ceremonial structures found in each village were the sites of these rituals, which included dancing and singing. Only tribal members who were fully initiated were allowed into the structure, while others celebrated outside. Ceremonial costumes consisted of a skirt and headdress or wig made of California condor feathers. Bodies were painted red, black or white. Tattoos were common among the native people of the Santa Ana Mountains, especially the women.

The remnants of stone structures have been discovered in the range, although little is known about their use or significance. It is possible that these merely marked out a sacred space or ceremonial location.

The sky was a mysterious place to the tribes of the Santa Ana Mountains. They believed that when people died, they turned into stars. Most California Indians, including those who lived in or near the range, feared falling stars, believing they carried evil spirits to the earth. During eclipses, the people would howl and scream, hoping to scare away the monsters that were eating the sun or moon.

The people of the Santa Ana Mountains were known to have kept time by using the sun and moon. Prior to construction of the Eastern Toll Road, a "Solstice Cave" was discovered. This cave was believed to measure the winter and summer solstices by lining up notches in the cave wall with the setting of the solstice sun over the isthmus of Catalina Island. Initial investigations showed this to occur on the winter solstice; unfortunately, the

Bedrock mortars like this one can be found throughout the range.

cave was destroyed to make way for the toll road prior to any in-depth study. Additionally, some artifacts were found in the cave to suggest that it was a place of ceremonial significance. It is likely that only the spiritual leaders of a tribe or clan would have been allowed in the cave. This sad occurrence is just one of many examples of modern society's disregard for our predecessors' history and heritage.

The clothing of the tribal groups was typical of most Southern California Indians. The men wore nothing, while the women wore front and rear aprons. Sandals made of yucca fiber were common among all people living in the Santa Ana Mountains.

Many descendants of the Juaneño, Gabrielino, Luiseno and Serrano people who lived in the Santa Ana Mountains still live in Southern California. Unfortunately, the U.S. government has not recognized many of the native tribes, and thus the lands that were sacred to them and in which they laid the bodies of their relatives is now being swallowed by overdevelopment and mismanagement. Many of these descendants have been struggling for official recognition and attempting to preserve their sacred heritage.

Signs of the rich native heritage can be found throughout the Santa Ana Mountains. The more we learn about the native peoples who explored the canyons, scaled the peaks and gathered life from the plants and animals of the Santa Ana Mountains, the easier it is to find their presence in the mountains today.

Black Star Canyon, the site of a notorious massacre of native people, is one such location. Today, the site is known as the Mariposa Preserve due to the many Mariposa lilies that grow there in the spring. It was previously known as Hidden Ranch and, for centuries before that, possibly called *Pahavugna* by the Tongva people who lived there, though I could find only one source for this name.

As the story goes, several of the Indians who lived in the village were blamed for stealing horses, so William Wolfskill and a posse of maybe ten others stormed the site and killed dozens of natives, including women and children. The massacre and its participants have in recent years been called into question. The descendants of Mr. Wolfskill have suggested that the letters, biographies and notes they have seen of William Wolfskill never mention the event, and thus they believe he may not have been involved. Today, Black Star Canyon has a sometimes dark reputation for spirits and such. Maybe the spirits of those who were gunned down remain?

Tenaja Canyon in the southern Santa Ana Mountains is another location where local indigenous people left their mark. Some hypothesize that it got its name from the deep bedrock mortars that remain along Tenaja Creek. Whether that is the namesake or not, Tenaja is a great example of how the combination of oak woodlands, water and other essentials like abundant game, medicinal plants and extensive views makes for great homes.

This mysterious maze rock was found in Bell Canyon and is now on display at Bowers Museum.

Chiquito Basin is another of the sites where bedrock mortars can be viewed by visitors to the range. Sitting beneath the shade of a dense live oak grove, it is easy to imagine the good life experienced by the people who inhabited the Santa Ana Mountains. Remember, though, that all native sites are sacred and must be treated as such. Do not, for any reason, take or move artifacts from where you find them. If you find a site or artifact that you want to know more about, photograph or draw a picture of it and call the Southern California Indian Center or the land manager for the land you are on.

CONQUISTADORES, PRIESTS AND VAQUEROS

The Spanish, like no other culture, have left a legacy on Southern California, and the Santa Anas have obtained more than a fair share of this legacy. The Spanish dominated Southern California for at least seventy-five years, until 1846, and even then their impact on the Santa Ana Mountains continued to a lesser extent for another one hundred years.

The first of the Spanish imperialists to actually visit the range was Gaspar de Portolá in 1769, more than two centuries after Juan Rodríguez Cabrillo first sailed past them in search of the great cities of gold. Portolá's party of priests and soldiers first encountered the range on Saint Anne's Day while

This grassy meadow is likely the location of the first Christian baptism in California. *Photo Courtesy of Bowers Museum.*

camped in Trabuco Canyon almost two weeks after leaving San Diego. The party subsequently named the canyon after one of the soldiers lost a "Trabuco" rifle in the dense canyon vegetation. And so the canyon has been named ever since.

The first baptisms in California are believed to have occurred at this time as the party made contact with the local native people. In a clearing in Cristianitos Canyon, the famed Padre Junípero Serra made Christians of people of Acjachemen or Payomkowishum ancestry.

The expedition continued north, spending at least one more night near the range along Santiago Creek. Although no longer in the Santa Ana Mountains, the expedition camped along the "River of the Sweetest Name of Jesus of Earthquakes," as it was named by Father Crespi, the party's journalist. Within moments, the soldiers of the expedition decided it would be more easily called the Santa Ana River, as they believed it flowed from the Santa Ana Mountains, which they had named just two days earlier.

While camped along the Santa Ana River, the Spanish had made introductions with the local natives whose village was on the opposite bank of the river. The tribal members, probably Tongva/Gabrielino, asked the Spanish to stay and make homes with them. Although the soldiers and priests declined the invitation, they agreed to return.

Among the explorers of that infamous expedition in 1769 were two of the dons who would eventually be the first Europeans to settle on the slopes of Old Saddleback. Men with names like Yorba and Serrano would join others like Grijalva, who came to the area with the Anza Expedition a few years later. None of these men stayed immediately; in fact, it would be almost twenty years before they officially made claim to the lands around the Santa Ana Mountains, but one can imagine the conversations around the campfire after seeing this new paradise.

About six years after originally visiting the area, the Spanish made good on their promise and returned to establish Mission San Juan Capistrano, famous for the swallows that return every year to nest in the rubble of the crumbling adobes.

In 1775, a bell and cross were raised on a hillside, believed by some historians to be near present-day Caspers Wilderness Park. Due to an Indian uprising at Mission San Diego, the priests and soldiers at San Juan Capistrano were called back to San Diego to help calm the natives and save the earlier mission. In 1776, Father Sera returned to Capistrano, eventually establishing the seventh mission in the California chain.

OLD MISSION CEMETERY

Situated on this hill, located between the two rivers of the Capistrano Valley, is this sacred and consecrated ground. From this hilltop, the ocean, Mission, and town can be seen. It is a perfect resting place for San Juan Capistrano's historic families. This cemetery dates back to the 1860's and was sold to the Catholic Church by James Sheehan, soon after his wife Ann's death in 1878. Native Acjachemen/Juaneno families from the early Rancho period, and later settlers to this Valley are buried here. On the headstones can be seen the names of those historic families who have been, and who still are, a part of San Juan Capistrano's rich history. This cemetery is owned by the Diocese of Orange and is operated by Mission San Juan Capistrano.

Old Mission Cemetery is located off Ortega Highway.

Historians differ on how they believe the local indigenous people came to live at the mission. Some suggest that the "Indians" were so enamored with the Spanish that they hypnotically wandered in and gave of themselves without resistance. Others suggest it was with complete force and disregard of the indigenous peoples' human rights. I tend to lean toward the latter but believe that, in all reality, it must have been some combination of those scenarios. There can be no argument, however, that the native culture, its languages and practices were systematically destroyed as a result of their internment at the Missions San Luis Rey, San Juan Capistrano and San Gabriel.

Metal slag was recently found in the furnaces of the Mission San Juan Capistrano, the oldest standing building in the state, which may show that the Juaneño were the first population in California to produce and use metal. Records also show that the Juaneños, during the mission era, practiced a form of placer mining in what is now Lucas Canyon and sold the recovered gold to the mission. Numerous gold and other mineral claims are still active in Lucas Canyon.

One of the legends of this time holds that a large cache of gold stolen from the mission after the earthquake of 1812 was hidden in the Santa Ana Mountains and never recovered. It is likely that this is a form of the legend of the pirate H. Bouchard, who raided the missions and settlements along the California Coast in the early nineteenth century.

As this story goes, or at least as I have heard it told, in 1818, Bouchard was heading north along the coast, and a rider came to warn the Mission at San Juan Capistrano. On hearing of the potential raid, priests took the mission's gold into the hills to hide it. When no word of safety came, the priests buried the gold and hung the keys to the gold chests on a nearby oak tree. Unfortunately, the priests never recorded where the gold was hidden. As the story goes, a pair of very old keys matching the description provided by the priests was recovered some 175 years later. Unfortunately, the finder of those keys failed to detail what tree the keys were recovered from, and the ranger to whom the keys were given failed to record the name and contact information of the finder. The ranger didn't know the story until sometime later. If you believe any of it, the gold still rests under an ancient oak tree in what is now Caspers Regional Park.

Whatever your feelings on the Mission at San Juan Capistrano's beginnings, its contribution to the history of the region and of the Santa Ana Mountains is indisputable. In fact, the most detailed description of the Acjachemen/ Juaneño and their early cultural practices that we have today was written by mission priest Father Geronimo Boscano in his "Historical Account of the Beliefs, Usages, Customs and Extravagancies of the Indians of the Mission San Juan Capistrano Called the Acjachemen Indians." In addition, most of the rancheros eventually settling the slopes and valleys beneath the Santa Ana Mountains were soldiers originally coming to the region to establish the missions and settle California in the name of Spain. Those families' names still grace cities, streets, buildings and natural landmarks.

The rancho era in Southern California is an important part of its rich history, but the Santa Ana Mountains were for the most part seen as a barrier—too steep, too dry and too hot. Rugged landscapes and a host of predators, including mountain lions, grizzly bears and a few wolves, were enough to keep even the hardiest of settlers in the foothills and plains. However, a few of the ranchos allowed their sheep and cattle to graze the slopes of the range and lower reaches of the mountains.

On the western slope of the range, Rancho Santiago de Santa Ana, Rancho Lomas de Santiago, Rancho Canada de los Alisos, Rancho Trabuco and Rancho Santa Margarita y las Flores were the most prominent. The lands belonging to the Mission San Juan Capistrano eventually became the Rancho Mission Viejo and also were on the western slopes.

The northern foot of the range was Rancho Canon de Santa Ana. The northeastern toe of the mountains near present-day Corona was Rancho La Sierra Yorba.

The eastern slopes fell into large holdings with names like Rancho Santa Rosa in the southeast portion of the range. Rancho La Laguna was around present-day Lake Elsinore, and Rancho Temescal ran much of the length of the eastern foot of the range. Life on the ranchos was by today's standards hard, at least for the Indian laborers who left the missions and moved onto the ranchos as laborers. And as was the custom of the times, they did most of the work. They cooked, tended the fields, gathered the cattle, cared for the children and built the homes of the rancheros. And for that they were fed, given shelter and paid a small wage. They raised their families on the ranchos and became highly skilled on horseback. They herded sheep and cattle and gathered medicinal herbs from the slopes of the Santa Ana Mountains.

Life on the ranches wasn't all work and no play. Fiestas were held regularly at roundup time, when all the regional ranchos would come together to sort out one another's cattle and to brand new calves. During this time, some typical rodeo-like events would take place and some not-so-typical ones as well. In fact, the term "rodeo" comes from the regular roundups and livestock counts that occurred on every rancho at least annually and sometimes seasonally. Between work, the vaqueros would show off their skills and hold friendly competitions with one another.

Although popular, the saddest of the entertainment was the bear versus bull fights that would occur on many of the ranchos around the Santa Anas. "Cowboys"—or more correctly, *vaqueros*—would go to the mountains to catch a griz, roping it and dragging it back to the rancho. The bears were then attached by rope or chain to the ranchos' biggest bull, and the two were forced to fight it out in the confines of a corral. Gruesome and cruel battles ensued as people enthusiastically looked on.

One of the Yorba Adobes is seen here. *Photo Courtesy of Bowers Museum.*

Although well documented and popular in our stories today, bull and bear fights were not common events. However, early California residents gathered regularly for the passion of the rancheros: horse racing. Fortunes were made and lost on the hoof of the horse. More than one vast parcel of land changed hands to pay off a racing debt. None of these races occurred in the Santa Ana Mountains, though the horses that ran them probably grazed the slopes of the range from time to time.

Teodocio Yorba, don of the Rancho Lomas de Santiago, was the most well known of the ranchero horse racers. His cousins and neighbors were active at betting the horses, but it was said of Teodocio that he loved to win but never seemed a sore loser when he didn't.

At one point, horses far outnumbered cattle on the slopes of Saddleback. The rancheros would graze large numbers of mares and their foals just as they would their cattle. A smaller number of horses were kept close to the home. Even today, the vaqueros of Old California are recognized for their legendary skill on and around horses. A few horse trainers even use the old ways to train horses today.

As many horses as there were on the old ranchos, banditos and horse thieves found a need to steal some more. Many of the first real documented ascents of the peaks, and descents into canyons, were recorded by those chasing horse thieves. One such chase took the posse into Coldwater Canyon and up Santiago Peak. Major Horace Bell, who led a band of Mormons and Angelino deputies, described in detail the wooded canyons, bears and awesome views from the top. They never caught up with the thieves, but the chase definitely went down in history as the first documented climb of Old Saddleback. It also is the namesake of Horsethief Trail.

Although by 1850 the Californians had gone from living under Spanish rule to Mexican control, and finally to membership in the rapidly expanding United States, life was still good for the rancheros and their families. But times were changing, and newcomers, speaking new languages with new customs, were on their way.

SETTLERS, STATEHOOD AND SHEEP

California became a state in 1850, officially ending the Spanish and Mexican eras and changing the landscape from one of ranchos to one of ranching and agriculture.

In the valleys below the Santa Ana Mountains, row crops were replacing wetlands, grasslands and sage scrub. Beets, beans and berries were being grown to feed the rapidly growing towns of Santa Ana, Orange and Anaheim. On the east side, development of any kind came slower, though the settlements of Corona and Lake Elsinore were growing.

While many took to the fields for livelihood, thousands of others were flocking to the canyons of the Santa Ana Mountains in search of wealth. Like most mountains in California, the Santa Anas were the site of several mining booms.

As early as 1862, Samuel Shrewsbury, the first to homestead in Santiago Canyon, was mining and burning lime in Limestone Canyon to be sold in the town of Santa Ana. Shrewsbury's home was in present-day Irvine Park and is believed to be the first non-adobe house in the region.

In 1876, coal was discovered in the Santa Ana Mountains, but since there was no immediate demand for coal at that time, the strike was almost forgotten. By 1878, however, as a result of the railroads' demand for coal, mines in the northern Santa Ana Mountains were hauling hundreds of wagons of coal to Santa Ana weekly. The coal's quality was low, and thus, so became the demand for it. A pile of the raw coal can still be seen today at the mouth of Fremont Canyon between Irvine Park and Irvine Lake. It is said that diamonds are merely coal that has been compressed over time. Check back cuz maybe the mining booms of the Santa Anas aren't over yet.

The town of Carbondale, in Silverado Canyon near the location of present-day Carbondale Ranch Stables, sprang out of the coal boom. Carbondale was preceded briefly by the town of Silverado, for which the canyon was named. In 1877, silver was discovered in Silverado Canyon, and the boomtown sprang up. The towns of Carbondale and Silverado were complete with post offices, saloons, hotels and general stores. Thousands of miners and the supporting staff flocked to the hills.

To keep the peace in the sometimes unruly mining towns, a government structure had to be set up. Samuel Shrewsbury was made justice of the peace, and Isaac Harding, another early settler for whom Harding Canyon is named, became chief constable.

By 1887, both the silver and coal booms were over, and the towns had all but disappeared. Nothing but a state historic plaque is left to mark the site of Carbondale. Silverado continued as a resort town for a few more years and exists as a rural canyon community today.

In the early 1900s, tin was apparently discovered in Trabuco Canyon, and mining began there. By 1907, the operation was shut down for good, with little or nothing to show for the years of work. Similar mining schemes occurred on the eastern slopes in, you guessed it, Tin Mine Canyon, though it seems that even more hoopla and less tin came from these claims.

Clay, gravel and the ingredients for cement manufacturing are the only mining operations of much scale in the Santa Anas today, although claims of many minerals, including silver, gold and tin, are still maintained. I even found a claim for uranium in the mountains, though no action has been taken on it. Many remnants from the early mining operations can still be found in the range.

Upper Santiago Canyon Mine Shaft.

Open shafts are common in some canyons, as are mining carts and other twisted metal remains.

The rancheros preferred cattle to graze their vast landholdings. Following the great droughts of 1863, when thousands of cattle died and many of the dons went bankrupt, smaller animals were called upon to graze what little grass grew back. Sheep were the livestock of choice for many new "ranchers" because they were easier to manage, and they ate more than grass. They were known to consume even the harshest and thorniest woody Chaparral plants. John Muir referred to sheep as "hooved locust" because of their ability to clear a landscape of all that grows. Abel Stearns and John Bixby ran sheep, as did the future king of the western slope, James Irvine.

In 1876, James Irvine Sr. obtained almost ninety-five thousand acres, or two complete ranchos and part of a third. In 1894, James Irvine Jr. created the Irvine Company to manage the huge ranch, which raised sheep and cattle, and grew beans, strawberries and citrus products. The Irvine Company controlled most of the foothills and western slopes of the Santa Anas and remains to this day the largest landowner in Orange County.

Other livelihoods of early settlers in the Santa Ana Mountains included beekeeping, of which Samuel Shrewsbury was again first. Honey attracted grizzly bears, and so bear hunting was also a pastime of early settlers in the range. The last griz in Southern California was killed in the Santa Ana Mountains in 1908.

Not all who came to the Santa Ana Mountains set up shop or home. In 1886, mountain man Jedediah Smith crossed the Santa Anas but continued on his way to the larger Coast Ranges to the north. Others who crossed the range had less than honest reasons for doing so.

The infamous bandit Juan Flores used the Santa Anas to hide in after raiding the ranches and homesteads of the Tustin Plain. In 1857, Flores shot and killed Sheriff John Barton and three deputies before being captured and hanged in Los Angeles. Flores Peak, near the mouth of Modjeska Canyon, is named after a shootout that took place there between Don Pico's Posse and the Flores Gang. Other bandits came to the Santa Ana Mountains and are remembered by such place names as Horsethief Canyon and Robbers Roost. Even the notorious Joaquin Murrieta hid out in the Santa Anas for a time.

Along with famous outlaws came famous lawmen. Perhaps the Wild West's most famous lawman, Wyatt Earp, spent a bit of time in the range. He is known to have frequented the east side, especially the Lake Elsinore area. His father, Nicholas Earp, lived in Bedford Canyon.

Earlier, in the late 1840s and '50s, John C. Fremont was a regular in the range. He was preparing the area for American rule, though many of the area's residents were not in support of it at first. Local legend holds that Fremont and his party of Americans lost a cannon and some cannonballs in lower Santiago Creek. To the best of my knowledge, this has never really been substantiated. I will always prefer to remember him for the Riparian tree named in his honor: the Fremont cottonwood.

With Fremont and the other soldiers came the infamous scout and tracker Kit Carson. His scouting ability in Southern California fell short of greatness, as he misinterpreted many of the actions of the Mexican and Spanish dons. He believed the laid-back nature of the rancheros meant they were ill prepared to defend their lands. As history demonstrated, it was paper, not bullets, that eventually did in the dons.

Some of the most feared of the mountains' residents are ghosts. *La Llorona* ("the Crier") lives along Trabuco Creek and is known for her crying screams. Legend holds that this woman drowned her three children in Trabuco Creek in order to have more time with her lover. She steals the souls of small children, and if you see her, according to the legend, you or someone close to you will die. Apparently, on moonlit nights, she can be seen looking in Trabuco Creek for her children. I reluctantly admit I have never seen her.

In recent years, the Tenaja area has gained minor fame for hosting strange visitors. Several UFO sightings have been reported in this area, and during the fall of 1992, while I was camped at Tenaja Campground, several unexplained lights were seen in the distant sky. Others at the campground had reported seeing these strange lights for several consecutive evenings. Nearly everybody with an opinion on the subject thinks the government is somehow involved. Some simply say it is a secret military plane being tested at the neighboring Camp Pendleton Marine Base. The marines emphatically deny this. Others say that aliens have chosen this place to subdue the military in case of an alien invasion. Whatever the reason for the lights, there is no denying that this is a popular place to see them.

A less mysterious population also came to the mountains, led by the likes of Helena Modjeska. A Polish-born actress, Madame Modjeska came to the Santa Anas in 1888 to establish an olive farm, although what she ended up with was peace of mind and a failing agricultural business. She stayed in the Santa Ana Mountains until illness forced her to relocate closer to civilization. Her beautiful home, which she named the Forest of Arden, is currently being managed as a historic park by the County of Orange and is open to the public. Her olive orchard still shades Modjeska Canyon Road today.

Ms. Modjeska also had a lasting impact on the native plants of the region. The caretaker of the Forest of Arden was Theodore Payne, and he took a great interest in the native plants of the Santa Ana Mountains, especially the wildflowers. He was an avid collector and recorder of the many species he saw. Today, the Theodore Payne Foundation is one of the best-known native plant nurseries and wildflower educational institutions in the state.

The search for solitude and peace of mind still brings people to the Santa Ana Mountains. A Krishna monastery has been established near Trabuco Canyon, allowing monks and other worshipers to meditate and pray in a natural and peaceful environment. Other spiritual and religious groups have also chosen the Santa Anas for their preferred site of worship. Although not officially part of any particular sect or religion, I, too, go up Old Saddleback for spiritual enlightenment. In the spirit of John Muir, I believe that the Santa Ana Mountains are one of "God's Greatest Temples." It is amazing how a day or two in the Santa Ana Mountains can make one forget about the stresses of life in the urban landscapes of Southern California. As I sit on top of Old Saddleback, I feel closer to God.

Although the Santa Ana Mountains backcountry remained relatively pristine, the federal government decided in 1892 to set a portion aside as a forest reserve. In 1908, it was changed to a national forest. Unlike many of the better-known forests, the Cleveland was not set aside to protect or provide timber supplies. Rather, the Santa Ana Mountains were added to the National Forest System to protect the vast watersheds of the range.

While for the most part the U.S. Forest Service has limited development within the watershed, it has also provided recreation facilities and allowed development of communication facilities (more than one hundred antennas and microwave dishes on Santiago Peak alone). Destruction of habitat within the national forest has been moderate and centered on a few areas. More questionable proposals have been placed on the table, including one that would drill a tunnel through the range to provide traffic relief to the freeways that already circumnavigate the range. Many conservation organizations support this proposal as the lesser of evils compared to a new freeway being cut into the mountains' pristine slopes and canyons.

Private land within the range has not been as lucky as that owned by the government. Development is the number one threat to the integrity of the Santa Ana Mountains. Even if all land within the national forest were preserved, many species of plants and animals could not survive. The Irvine and Santa Rosa Ranches, two of the largest landowners in the range, have for more than three decades been converting land from agriculture to commercial and residential development. Citizen activism is essential for the preservation of cultural resources and viable ecosystems in the Santa Ana Mountains.

The Twentieth Century

No century in the twelve-million-year history of the Santa Ana Mountains has had a greater impact on the range than did the twentieth century. Cars, communication and cultural changes have influenced the range in obvious and subtle ways.

Perhaps many of the most profound changes of the early twentieth century were made on paper in the halls of government rather than actually on the slopes of Old Saddleback. Creation of the National Forest System is one such example. Although the Trabuco Forest Preserve was originally founded in the late 1800s, it was made into the Trabuco National Forest in

1906, and then, in 1908, the protected area was nearly doubled and added to the Cleveland National Forest.

Unlike the national forests of the north, the Trabuco District was set aside to protect watersheds rather than timber. Timber was harvested from a few of the canyons in the northern range into the 1900s, but it was never a major industry because the supply was limited. Severe floods followed by drought and then again by floods were the standard then as now, and overgrazing, fire and poor construction engineering wreaked havoc on the slopes and creeks of the Santa Ana Mountains.

Local cowboys, or more likely vaqueros, were hired to patrol the range in search of illegal grazing and for fire prevention efforts. They were paid $600 per year; however, as many worked the range only seasonally, their salaries were paid monthly. Unlike government workers of today, the rangers were required to use all of their own gear, including horses, saddles and camping supplies. But it was a good life for the last of the region's cowpunchers. Most of the big ranches were being converted to row crops and cities; even those that were still grazing were doing so in smaller allotments, and fences were being put up to keep animals on site. Ranger work was a wanderer's life, and it suited the old cowboys well—though more changes would soon end that lifestyle, too.

Two great ranches impacted the western slopes of the Santa Ana Mountains, and these were the Irvine Ranch at approximately 100,000 acres and what would eventually become the Rancho Mission Viejo at a staggering 200,000 acres. The story of the former is well told, while the latter has slipped by almost silently into the twenty-first century.

The land was originally granted in 1845 to Juan Forester and consisted of three ranchos: the Rancho Santa Margarita y las Flores, the Rancho Trabuco and the Rancho Mission Viejo. Together, these properties covered 200,000 acres of the western slopes of the Santa Ana Mountains all the way to the ocean. In 1907, James Flood and Richard O'neill Sr. joined forces to purchase and consolidate the three ranchos, with Flood being the financer and O'neill the rancher. In 1923, the properties were all consolidated under the name the Santa Margarita Company, but it would prove to be short lived. In 1939, the property was divided among the heirs of the Flood and O'neill families. Richard O'neill Jr. received the property on the Orange County side of the line, which totaled approximately 52,000 acres, and the Flood family received the San Diego County side of the ranch at approximately 125,000 acres. The San Diego County property was purchased in 1942 by the U.S. government to expand Camp Pendleton Marine Corps Base. The remaining lands in Orange County became known as Rancho Mission Viejo

A modern view of the Rancho Mission Viejo.

and the Mission Viejo Company. It remains a cattle and farming operation on nearly 20,000 acres today, although it is best known for the residential communities it built. We now know the lands as the cities of Mission Viejo and Ladera Ranch.

It was during the 1900s that roads were built into and around the Santa Ana Mountains, making access to the once rugged and foreboding mountains easier. Almost all of the roads in the range were originally constructed by the Civilian Conservation Corps, and most followed the paths of early trails. Some of those trails dated back to pre-Columbian times.

Ortega Highway is the only paved road to cross the range, and it follows an ancient trading route used by the Acjachemen and Payomkowishum Indians to trade with their neighbors to the east. The highway was first constructed between 1929 and 1933, although "the mountain road" out of Elsinore was constructed by horse teams and hand crews more than ten years earlier. The highway has been "improved" several times since its construction. However, having lived just off the highway in El Cariso Village, I know firsthand that the road is limited, even today, in its ability to carry the heavy load of traffic that plies its lanes every day. Just one small fender bender in the afternoon can strand thousands of people in San Juan Capistrano, with the only alternative routes adding one hundred miles to their journey. All one has to do is hike the path of San Juan Creek, which serves as a graveyard of broken and bent vehicles as it guides the highway above, to see that there have been more than just small fender benders along this highway. On one such exploration, I was able to identify a car from every decade from the 1960s through 2000.

The CCC built many unpaved roads too. In fact, nearly every truck trail in the Santa Ana Mountains was built by conservation workers in between 1933 and 1941. The public works projects included many skilled trades as well. Their works are evident in Irvine's regional park, where attractive rock and masonry walls and flood channels were constructed. Similar themes were carried out all the way down Santiago Creek and are still evident in city parks like Hart Park and Santiago Park in Orange and Santa Ana, respectively. Once you know CCC style, you can find it all over, including in several of the campgrounds in the range. Upper San Juan Campground was constructed by the Conservation Corps, as was Falcon Group Camp and Blue Jay Campground above Los Pinos.

Conservation crews built fire lookouts on Santiago Peak and above Tenaja in the southern part of the range. They installed erosion control projects and firebreaks. CCC projects are evident in Trabuco, Silverado and Modjeska Canyons as well. Although long since washed away or removed by hand, there were once four U.S. Forest Service–operated campgrounds in Trabuco Canyon. Today, only O'neill Regional Park provides camping in the vicinity of Trabuco Canyon.

By 1920, the Santa Ana Mountains were on regional and federal recreation agendas. Populations of nearby cities were growing, and the desire of people to explore and commune with nature was expanding rapidly. As a result, the Santa Anas became a destination for many seeking recreational opportunities.

There once were more than seventy recreational cabins in Trabuco Canyon and more in Holy Jim, Silverado, Hot Springs and San Juan Canyons. All were constructed between 1920 and 1965, but floods and a

The Santa Anas have been a popular recreational destination since the late 1800s.

change in the federal land lease program brought an end to the summer cabin program by 1966. Many of the cabins not destroyed by flood, fire or vandalism became full-time residences and continue to be occupied today. Others remain vacation properties used seasonally.

As the Santa Ana Mountains became more popular, many of the ranges' existing residents were forced out. Among them were the major predators of the food chain. Wolves, jaguars and grizzly bears were all extirpated from the Santa Ana Mountains by 1920. Although officially gone, regular reports of bear and even one of jaguars have been recorded, though sometimes those records are only stored on a stool at the bar at Cooks Corner or in a booth at the Silverado Café. Though the bear reports are not of grizzlies, many black bears have been spotted in the range but remain, like ghosts, only unofficially believed to exist here.

As a result of the demise of many of the range's plants and animals, people began to recognize the importance of studying the Santa Ana Mountains. Perhaps the most important of the early studies was conducted by Willis E. Pequagnat, beginning in 1937 and running through 1941. This landmark study produced the "Biota of the Santa Ana Mountains," a book-sized dissertation on everything encountered over those years of intense field study.

Pequagnat was able to paint the big picture of conditions in the Santa Ana Mountains, whereas, up to this time, only the conditions of single canyons or properties were being monitored. The "Biota of the Santa Ana Mountains" has become the baseline for Santa Ana Mountain conservation. In fact, in many ways, that study has influenced me to write this book. I regularly return to it for information on what was here before me, and I know that many other researchers also rely on Pequagnat's compilation some seventy years after it was recorded.

Little Black Bear, shown here after death, was the last of the Santa Ana Mountain grizzlies.

The "Biota" also inspired the Santa Ana Mountain Ecosystem Expedition, which lasted only about six weeks but aimed to retrace the original study. The latter expedition ended in the creation of a documentary film titled *The Santa Ana Mountains: True Stories of a Great Range.*

Willis Pequagnat wasn't the only person who spent the twentieth century closely watching the Santa Ana Mountains. Terry Stephenson and Jim Sleeper both published books on the range and regularly wrote and spoke about the mountains. Stephenson's classic book, *In the Shadows of Old Saddleback*, first published in 1931, was the first effort at recording the cultural heritage of the people living in the Santa Ana Mountains and making it available for public consumption.

Later, in 1976, Sleeper published the humorous and often tall tales of the range in his book *A Boy's Book of Bear Stories*. Sleeper, who became widely recognized as one of Orange County's premier historians and the official historian of the Irvine Ranch, lived much of his life at a cabin deep in Trabuco Canyon. Jim Sleeper passed away in 2012 during the writing of this book, but his contribution to the knowledge and historical record of the Santa Ana Mountains is undeniable and, hopefully, is carried on in this book.

About the same time that Jim Sleeper was writing about the history of the range, another gentleman, Kenneth Croker, was writing about the present Santa Ana Mountains. Ken was a trail volunteer for the Sierra Club, and through his years of building and repairing trails, he recognized the importance of the Santa Ana Mountains as a recreational resource. His guide, simply titled *Santa Ana Mountains Trail Guide*, was a must-have for the author's generation of local mountain men and explorers. It made getting into the Santa Ana Mountains reasonable, whereas without the book, there was just a collection of poorly signed gates and private property signs. I can only hope that the book you are reading does as much to introduce a new generation to the mountains as Croker's book did for my generation.

Although the Santa Ana Mountains had their guardians, they were no match for the forces that saw the mountains as only a utilitarian resource. These forces included water districts, communications companies and power generators and distributors among their ranks. In most cases, these powerful entities used fear to move their agendas and projects forward; however, in some cases they just built them with little or no oversight or public participation.

One such example of the just-build-it mentality was the construction of dams. Property owners throughout the Santa Anas pushed dirt into piles to block the flow of the little creeks or poured concrete to block larger flows. Most of these were built to provide irrigation or water for livestock and were always considered temporary infrastructure. My favorite example of dams in the Santa Ana Mountains is near the bottom of Harding Canyon. As hikers descend the north slope from the crest between Modjeska and Harding Canyon off the Harding Truck Trail and into Harding Canyon, a wide, flat canyon floor opens up. The area has braided stream channels (though they are often dry channels) that wind in and out of sycamore groves. The site is easily mistaken for one of ancient history as the sandy bottom meets the sandstone walls of the canyon. However, for explorers who turn down the canyon and walk another quarter mile, they realize that the ground they are standing on is sediment deposited over only fifty years of flows and that they are standing at the top of what was once a dam designed to hold backwater. Today, it merely holds back the sand as water flows over its top, providing a beautiful waterfall for the residents below.

Another, better-planned dam is that of Santiago Reservoir or what today is known as Irvine Lake. This body of water is now the largest watering hole in the Santa Ana Mountains. Construction on the earthen dam began in 1929 and was completed in 1931. The lake was constructed to provide irrigation water to the crops of the Irvine Ranch and other farms fed by the Serrano Irrigation District. By the end of 1931, the dam and its partner, Santiago Creek, had done their jobs, and the lake had filled to cover more than seven hundred acres or twenty-eight thousand acre feet of water.

The dam was stocked with fish and opened to the public in 1941. Today, it remains a popular fishing destination, and in addition to providing irrigation waters, it also provides drinking water to the communities of Villa Park and Orange.

Perhaps the most obvious of the modern changes to the Santa Ana Mountains are the installations of communications towers and antennas on many of the peaks in the range. These are necessary eyesores—visible for many miles and from all sides of the range—that have prevented the mountains from being recognized for their wild and scenic beauty. That being said, the towers also allow the millions of residents living at the foot of the mountains to communicate with one another and to have secure emergency services provided to them. Leases have been handed out to many media companies, as well, allowing us all to enjoy radio, television and internet broadcasting.

One tower that commands attention for its unique design is the Doppler radar tower above the head of Fremont Canyon. This white tower that appears to have a giant golf ball on top can be seen from both sides of the range and has often been the topic of questions among guests I have led through the northern Santa Ana Mountains and their vicinity. This tower allows meteorologists to view multidimensional radar images of the approaching weather systems and provide better current reports and predictions regarding the weather for the Greater Los Angeles area. Today, approximately three hundred towers and antennas dot the peaks and ridges of the Santa Ana Mountains.

Almost as obvious and equally as damaging to the scenic quality of the Santa Ana Mountains has been the installation of power transmission lines. Huge towers cross the range in several places, including near Ladd Canyon, which has prevented that area from receiving special designation such as Wilderness. The large towers have become dangerous for planes and helicopters flying over the range. In one location near Coal Canyon, the towers and lines stretch across the Santa Ana Canyon and are marked with colorful balls to prevent them from being clipped by aircraft.

As important as electricity is to most of us, the Santa Ana Mountains were home to a few characters who had no need for such things. One such spirit is called to mind by anyone who explores the northern Main Divide Road or climbs to the top of Black Star Canyon. Here we find a sort of monument to freedom, the pioneering spirit and a family that has known and loved the Santa Ana Mountains more than most. Known officially as Beeks Place, the stone ruins here date back decades to the 1930s, when Joseph Beek and his family built the one-room house, a smaller caretaker's cabin, ponds and other facilities on the property. They planted trees and spent many weekends "on the Mountain." The Beek family was known to inhabit the buildings without fully running water, electricity and other luxuries most of us take for granted. The Beek family still owns the full section, or 640 acres, that surround the property, although they have been seeking a buyer for some time. Unlike most property owners, however, the Beeks are not just seeking a lot of money; they also want the right buyer, as the Santa Ana Mountains are still an important resource of historical value for their family.

In recent times, and as late as the writing of this book, the remaining Beek family members have allowed Naturalist For You, a tremendous environmental education and conservation nonprofit organization, to begin cleaning up and restoring the property. The hope is that eventually Beeks Place can be fully restored and turned into a northern Santa Ana Mountains field station. It has always been my vision and dream that field stations be established at Beeks in the north and at the Old Tenaja ranger station in the south. These would make great locations for educational programming, ecological and recreational research and so much more.

Not to be outdone, Mother Nature made her presence known in the twentieth century. In the winter of 1937 and 1938, she opened the floodgates, and the Santa Ana Mountains were swept up in a current of water that left true devastation in its path. Hardest hit was Trabuco Canyon, where cabins and campgrounds were completely washed away. Bridges and roads were devoured as creek banks disappeared under unexpected flows.

The flood of 1938 was just a warning shot, however, because thirty-one years later Mother Nature really let the mountains have it. The floods of 1969 are considered the worst modern flooding event in Southern California's history. Though there have been larger floods, there was less damage and fewer losses. Again, Trabuco Canyon was washed over in a torrent of water, but this time Modjeska and Silverado Canyons also suffered great damage. The Dams at Santiago Reservoir (Irvine Lake) and Villa Park were topped, and Santiago Creek rushed out of the mountains and into the cities below, taking homes, cars and people with it. New stream channels were carved, hillsides slipped and old canyon bottoms were filled. The flood of 1969 carried the Santa Ana Mountains into the modern era of engineering and management. Land managers haven't looked back since.

Even conservation efforts took a turn toward the industrial at the end of the twentieth century. In the 1990s, California and the federal government teamed up to test a new community approach to the conservation of endangered species. They called it the Natural Community Conservation Planning Program, and it was supposed to look at entire ecosystems and plan the future of those areas. The Santa Ana Mountains and western foothills were to be the first run of this program.

The government argued that by looking at the needs of multiple species simultaneously, they could plan for the future of those species and development simultaneously. Conservationists were slow to get on board with the program, especially since many of those species had already been designated as threatened or endangered under the state or federal endangered species acts. Activists believed and argued in court that if those species received the protection granted under the Endangered Species Act, this new program was unnecessary and circumvented the law. The government prevailed, and the Natural Community Conservation Plan was put into action. Today, thousands of acres known as the Central Orange County reserve protect the California gnatcatcher, orange-throated whiptail, coastal cactus wren and dozens of other plants and animals in the Santa Ana Mountains and foothills. It is still too soon to say that it protects these species better than the Endangered Species Act would have, but the Santa Ana Mountains are better for the planning effort.

PART II

Habitats

The rugged topography, geographic location and relatively limited human impacts make the Santa Ana Mountains a biological treasure rich in diversity of plants, animals and natural communities. Recognized by even the most conservative ecologists as the last intact coastal ecosystem in Southern California, the slopes of Old Saddleback are an important reserve of biological information and history. Even well into the twenty-first century, there are places in these mountains that have not been studied or inventoried. I have included some of my own personal experiences and journal recollections to help illustrate the biological wonder that is the Santa Ana Mountains.

LIFE ZONES AND NATURAL COMMUNITIES

Since well before the beginning of recorded history, humans have attempted to classify everything around them as a means of understanding it. Nature has not escaped this classification, and over the last 150 years, several methods of categorizing units of our environment have arisen.

In the late 1800s, C. Hart Merriam, who studied the remains of grizzly bears killed in the Santa Ana Mountains, devised the life zone concept after walking from the Grand Canyon to the top of the San Francisco Peaks, Arizona's highest point. He found that certain elevations showed clear differences in vegetation types and that there were similarities between elevation and latitude. Merriam decided on six life zones and named them after geographic areas with like climates. The life zones described by Merriam were named Lower and Upper Sonoran, Transition, Canadian, Hudsonian and Arctic/Alpine.

The Santa Ana Mountains are almost entirely in the Upper Sonoran life zone. The peaks of Old Saddleback, however, reach into the Transition zone. Unfortunately, the life zone concept can be applied with much accuracy only to the southwest United States.

Because of the diversity of habitats in California, ecologists needed a more detailed system of classification. In the 1950s, botanists Phillip Munz and David Keck devised the plant communities system, which has been in widespread use ever since. This system divides communities into groups based on the most common plants in an area. A variation of this system is used here and separates the range into eight plant communities. Sometimes these are also referred to as natural communities. These natural communities became the basis of the Natural Community Conservation Planning Program, which is responsible for the preservation of thousands of acres within the Greater Santa Ana Mountains Ecosystem:

Southern California (Valley) Grassland
Coastal Sage Scrub
Chamise Chaparral
Broadleaf Chaparral
Southern Oak Woodland
Riparian Woodland
Conifer Forest
Vernal Pool Ephemeral

Comparing the life zone and plant community classification concepts allows us to draw some correlations between plant species and elevation. This connection makes the hundreds of plants found in the Santa Ana Mountains and their relationship to slope, aspect and soil all make a little more sense. Below are descriptions of the plants and locals that make up the eight plant communities and a few of the sub-communities that make up the Santa Ana Mountains.

The view from the top of Ladd Canyon looks toward Silverado Canyon.

Southern California (Valley) Grassland

Originally, this community consisted purely of native California bunchgrasses, but since the introduction of livestock, it has been taken over in most places by introduced annual grasses. There are probably fewer than ten thousand acres of this community in the Santa Ana Mountains. Limestone Canyon, Irvine Mesa and the Santa Rosa Plateau are locations to see great stands of native grasses.

Purple needle grass is the most common native species in the range, though several others are found here as well. Wild oats are one of the most common introduced species.

Coastal Sage Scrub

More than thirty thousand acres of coastal sage scrub exist in the Santa Ana Mountains in a complex pattern of public and private ownership. This

65

habitat exists nowhere else in the world but Southern California, and as much as 95 percent has already been degraded by urban sprawl, overuse and mismanagement.

This aromatic blend of woody and herbaceous shrubs consists of California (coastal) sagebrush, several species from the mint family, including white sage and black sage. Purple sage is a member of this community but finds its southern range limits in the Santa Ana Mountains around Black Star and Fremont Canyons. California buckwheat and monkey flower join the other more common plants of the community. Coastal cholla and prickly pear cactus are found in a subcommunity of coastal sage scrub that is important to animals such as the cactus wren. Toyon and lemonade berry are common in coastal sage scrub on north-facing slopes. Coastal sage scrub is sometimes referred to as "soft chaparral" because of its somewhat lower growth habit and more open structure that allows for limited navigation. It also tends to have fewer thorns and spines than plants found in the Chaparral communities. Many of the plants found

in the coastal sage scrub community are drought deciduous, meaning they lose their leaves in periods of drought but can grow them back rapidly following precipitation.

Once found from the coast to about three thousand feet in the Santa Ana Mountains, much of this community has been replaced by houses, roads and industrial centers. The Santa Ana Mountains and related foothills make up the bulk of the remaining Coastal Sage Scrub habitat. More than one hundred species of plants and animals that depend on this community for survival are at some level threatened with extirpation or complete extinction.

Coastal sage scrub covers much of the Santa Ana Mountains below three thousand feet.

Chamise Chaparral

Chamise is the most common plant in low-elevation Chaparral, and in terms of biomass it is one of the most abundant plants in California. In the Santa Ana Mountains, it is especially common on south-facing slopes, where it is often found in pure stands. Chamise is adapted to fires, sprouting immediately after burning. Other plants associated with lower Chaparral include the California lilac or *Ceonothus* species. Sometimes, the slopes of the Santa Ana Mountains are covered in a blue, purple or white scene when the *Ceonothus* blooms. Trips over Ortega Highway are a good way to experience this colorful annual event. Scrub oak and holly-leaved red berry are common on north slopes in lower Chaparral. This community extends from just above three thousand feet to about five thousand feet elevation.

Several landowners in Central and Northern California have experimented with making charcoal from chamise. This would add economic value to one of the state's most common plants. Though this may not be an entirely good thing, it may change many people's view of a misunderstood plant and one of the region's most important plant communities.

Broadleaf Chaparral

Several species of manzanita, mountain mahogany and scrub oak represent the most abundant species in the Upper Chaparral community. Upper chaparral, or broadleaf chaparral, grows in the Santa Ana Mountains from about four thousand feet to the peaks of Old Saddleback, well above five thousand feet.

Many of the plants in this community are sun trackers, meaning the leaves of these plants turn with the sun. The leaves are also sclerophyllous, or leather-like, thick and dense to slow the loss of water.

Southern Oak Woodland

This woodland community is made up of several species of oak, California sycamore, some California black walnut and other species of trees. Coast live oak is the most common oak in the Santa Ana Mountains; however, canyon live oaks, interior live oaks and Engelmann oaks may all be found in Southern Oak Woodlands. The understory in this community consists primarily of grasses and herbaceous plants. Rarely very dense, this community is common on north-facing slopes, flats and canyon bottoms.

Riparian Woodland

A moisture-dependent community, this is one of the most important habitats in the western United States. This community occurs along drainages with surface flow for at least part of the year. Willow, cottonwood, big-leaf maple, alder and mule fat are some of the trees and shrubs found in this community within the Santa Ana Mountains. Because of the presence of water, a dense understory is often associated with this community. Many of our wild berries and grapes can be found in Riparian communities, as can be poison oak. Some estimates suggest that as much as 90 percent of Southern California's Riparian habitat is gone or in poor condition.

This riparian forest in San Mateo Canyon is typical of many canyon bottoms.

Conifer Forest

As many as five sub communities of Conifer Forest grow in the Santa Ana Mountains. Because many of these are isolated stands that cover relatively little acreage, I have combined them into one general community heading. Closed-cone forests in the range consist of knob cone pine and Tecate cypress forests.

The knob cone pine stands are restricted to serpentine soil around Pleasants Peak. These stands represent the southernmost stands of knob cone pine in the state.

The Tecate cypress stands are located on the northwest slopes of Sierra Peak in Coal and Gypsum Canyons. These trees exist on acidic soil, which discourages chaparral from becoming established. As mentioned earlier, Tecate cypress requires fire every three or four decades for reproduction. The Santa Ana Mountains stands of Tecate cypress include the largest and oldest specimens.

Coulter pines make up the third sub community of Conifer Forest in the Santa Ana Mountains and are probably the most abundant conifer in the range. The largest stands of Coulter pines in the range are found along the crest south of Modjeska Peak. Seeds from these cones were once collected as a food source by indigenous people. Large stands of this tree species were logged in the 1800s to build the mines and supporting buildings that created the boomtowns of Silverado and Carbondale during the silver and coal booms of the late 1800s.

Big-cone Douglas fir forests make up another of the sub communities of the Conifer Forest category. Big-cone Dougs tend to prefer the wetter, coastal-facing slopes in canyons. Pacific madrone and coast live oak are

The conifer forests in Trabuco Canyon make visitors feel like they are hundreds of miles north of Orange County.

closely associated with the Douglas fir sub community. Some of the largest stands of big-cone Douglas fir are found in the Santa Ana Mountains.

Monterey pines have been planted throughout the range as reforestation projects. These trees have become quite large in some places and appear to be natural, not planted.

Vernal Pool Ephemeral

Vernal Pool Ephemeral is probably the most unique community in the range. The pools fill with water during winter rains but begin drying out as soon as spring arrives. Unlike ordinary puddles or ponds, the retreating waters in a vernal pool reveal a brilliant, multicolored array of wildflowers and a unique cast of invertebrates. More than a dozen vernal pools, most of which are within the Santa Rosa Plateau Preserve, can be found in the Santa Ana Mountains. Interesting plant species of this community include the rare Orcutt grass, Parish's meadow foam and a couple species from the genus *Downingia*.

The communities described above are simply ways to help us better identify and understand a place. I hope that we have achieved that goal.

LAS FLORES (THE FLOWERS)

From a distance, the Santa Ana Mountains appear to be covered in a low-growing monoculture, but on closer investigation, their true floral diversity is revealed. In fact, more than 340 species have been identified and form at least eight vegetation communities.

In those eight communities, a dozen species grow that cannot be found anywhere else on earth. They grow in unique microhabitats that have evolved over hundreds of thousands of years. Many other plant species are at the limits of their respective ranges on the slopes of Old Saddleback and its adjoining peaks, ridges and canyons.

The Santa Ana Mountains, much to the surprise of first-time visitors, even have some of the world's most intriguing forests. For instance, some of the largest and last remaining stands of Engelmann oak are found in the plateaus of the southern range. These large, spreading oaks resemble the coast live oak but have a less dense crown and foliage than their more common cousins.

In addition, the largest and oldest Tecate cypress trees in the world grow in the Santa Ana Mountains near the ridge at the top of Coal and Gypsum Canyons. Several fires have burned this area in the last decade, and many of the trees in this grove have suffered. Normally, a fire benefits the Tecate cypress because its cones do not open to release seeds until they have reached extremely high temperatures only possible with a fire. Unfortunately, the Tecate cypress doesn't produce viable seeds until the trees have reached twenty-five to thirty years of age. Too many fires means no more Tecate cypress trees.

One of the largest stands of big-cone Douglas fir grows in Trabuco Canyon, making much of the experience in this canyon feel like one from the Northwest, not Southern California. Furthering that feeling is the southernmost stand of madrone trees in the same canyon. Madrone is common in the redwood region.

Other unique habitats and interesting floral occurrences include serpentine soils with knob cone pines, a hybrid oak with only one of the parent plants present in the range and more than a dozen increasingly rare vernal pools.

Because an entire book would be required to describe every species of plant that grows in the Santa Ana Mountains, I have chosen to limit the list to about one hundred of the most common wildflowers, fungi, ferns, shrubs and trees found in the range. Besides, a fantastic book on the flora of the Santa Ana Mountains is currently in the works. I am not a botanist; rather, I am a generalist who is willing to let the complex details be explained by someone else. I have, however, seen excerpts from the work, and it will be well worth the money. With that in mind, remember that sometimes it is not enough to just see the flowers. Every so often, one should get down on all fours and greet them nose-to-petal.

Following are descriptions of about one hundred plants found in the range. Several categories are presented to assist the reader in locating an individual plant within this guide. Miscellaneous Plants includes fungi, even though they really aren't plants at all, and ferns, as well as some of the more peculiar species like dodder and mistletoe. Wildflowers is the second category and consists of twenty-five of the most common showy plants in the range. The final two sections of this chapter are based on structure and height. Shrubs and trees are described in these sections.

Miscellaneous Plants

FUNGI

Fungi are not plants; in fact, they are a kingdom of their own. The mushrooms we commonly think of as fungi are actually fruit-like structures from much larger organisms usually found beneath the soil. Following are descriptions for some of the most common mushrooms in the range and their habitats.

Golden milk cap (Lactarius insulsus). This sometimes large, white and yellowish-brown mushroom is found only in live oaks.

Many-colored polypore (Coriolus versicolor). A shelf-like fungus with various colored rings. Found on logs, stumps and fallen branches of live oaks.

Oyster mushroom (Pleurotis esteatus). These white mushrooms vary widely but are known for their crescent-shaped caps. This species is associated with live oaks, cottonwoods, alders and sycamores.

Ruassula emetica. These grow two inches high, with red umbrella-like caps and white undersides and stalks. Hosts for this fungi include oaks, madrone, manzanita and pine.

FERNS

Like fungi, some plants also reproduce with spores rather than seeds. Following are some examples of the spore-producing plants in the Santa Ana Mountains.

Coastal wood fern (Dryopteris arguta). This wood fern is found in moist, shady woodlands below five thousand feet. Several fronds rise from the base. Blades are lance shaped and toothed. This is a relatively common fern in the Santa Ana Mountains.

Coffee fern (Pallaea andromedaefolia). These are usually fairly small, found in shaded, rocky outcrops. They have alternately branching fronds. Foliage is round to oblong and curling underneath, resembling coffee beans. Color is green to purplish brown.

Common horsetail (Equisetum arvense). Usually less than two feet high, the horsetail has a single stalk with needle-like sheaths growing in whorls from it. Sheaths sometimes are not present. Spores are produced on cone-like structures. Horsetail grows in wet soil and sometimes in shallow water. Fossil records show that horsetail trees up to fifty feet high once covered much of the earth in dense, moist forests.

Maidenhair fern (Adiantum jordanii). A unique-looking fern with alternately branched fronds. Foliage is round to ovate, with the outer edge toothed and/ or parted. Maidenhair is found throughout the range on moist, shaded slopes.

These giant chain ferns in Trabuco Canyon are one of the many fern species in the range.

OTHER MISCELLANEOUS PLANTS

Many plants in the Santa Ana Mountains are of interest for their growth form, structure or unique adaptations. The following descriptions are of flowering plants known for reasons other than their blooms, which may or may not be showy. Vines and parasites are included here.

Chalk dudleya (Dudleya parvarulenta). This is the most common of the live-forevers and is named for the chalky film that covers its broad gray-green leaves with sharp, pointed tips. This species can grow to more than a foot wide and is found on slopes, rock outcrops and canyon walls.

Dodder (Cuscuta californica). A common parasitic plant lacking chlorophyll. It has yellow or orange twining and a hair-like vine. Common throughout the range, it often colors entire hillsides with a golden hue.

Chalk *Dudleya* can be found in rock outcrops and canyon walls.

Lance-leaved Live Forever (Dudleya lanceolata). A green, leathery succulent with plump lance-shaped leaves growing in a rosette. Waxy flowers are clustered at the end of a red or orange nearly leafless stalk up to two feet long. Common on slopes and canyon walls throughout the range.

Mistletoe (Phoradendron villosum). A parasite. This species is most common on oaks. Its leaves are elliptical or obvate, and its flowers are very small and fruits berry-like. Dull green in color, it is spread by birds, especially phainopepla.

Wild cucumber (Marah macrocarpus). This attractive vine grows from a huge root and is known as the manroot plant as well as wild cucumber. Palmately lobed leaves three to four inches wide grow from trailing stems several feet long. Flowers are off-white, and both male and female flowers occur on the same plant. Large oval fruits are bright green when young,

Lance-leaf *Dudleyas* prefer moister habitats but are also found on rocks and cliff sides.

covered in soft spines. As the plant dries and turns brown, the spines become sharp and brittle. No part of this plant is edible, despite its name.

Wildflowers

The late, great American folk singer and storyteller Woody Guthrie called California the "Garden of Eden." A hike in the Santa Ana Mountains in late March could convince even the most skeptical that this was true. But don't wait for spring because almost any time or season in the range is a good time for flowers.

Following are descriptions of some of the most common and showy wildflowers found in the Santa Ana Mountains. Some are tiny herbs that will require us to get down on our hands and knees, while others are shrubs that may tower above us ten feet or more. They are grouped by the color of their blossoms instead of the families they belong to. The groups are: Blue/Purple, Yellow/White and Red/Orange. Remember, though, nature is not so uniform, and some flowers (e.g. lupines), may be described in another section.

BLUE/PURPLE

Blue dicks (Dichelostemma pulchella). A common perennial, blue dicks have long, narrow, parallel-veined blade-like leaves growing from the base of the plant and a noticeable keel along the underside. Numerous purple or blue funnel-shaped flowers radiate from the end of a single stalk. Leaves often disappear before flowers bloom. They are found mostly in open grassy areas.

Blue-eyed grass (Sisyrinchium bellum). This species' leaves are parallel veined, much like blades of grass. Its bluish purple flowers have yellow centers. Plants are about one-foot high. Blue-eyed grass is common in Valley Grassland and Coastal Sage Scrub.

Lupine (Lupinus species). A dozen species of lupine can be found in the Santa Ana Mountains, as annual or perennial herbs or small shrubs. Leaves are palmately compound and gray-green to bright green. Flowers are usually purplish blue but can be white or yellow also. Twelve to thirty flowers are whorled along a stock and resemble other pea flowers to which lupines are related. A popular old naturalist's tale is that if the lupines are blooming, the snakes have come out. I can't ever remember seeing a rattlesnake, in particular, before the lupines have bloomed.

Many lupine species are found in the Santa Ana Mountains.

Mariposa lily (Calochortus splendens). This is the most common mariposa lily in the range. It has a pale lavender–colored flower, usually with a purple spot near the base. Basal leaves are long and very narrow. It's found in Valley Grassland and Chaparral throughout the range. The Wildlands Conservancy recently purchased Hidden Ranch in Black Star Canyon and renamed the area the Mariposa Preserve because of the spectacular mariposa lily blooms that occur there every year. *Mariposa* means "butterfly" in Spanish. You can imagine how this lily got its name.

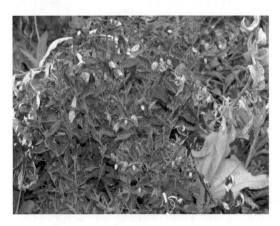

Coast paintbrush mingled with sage.

Periwinkle (Vinca major). A trailing, evergreen groundcover, periwinkle has dark-green, ovate leaves and solitary, violet-blue flowers. It was introduced to the West and the Santa Ana Mountains by early settlers. A telltale sign of past human habitation, this species is often found in canyons covering the foundations of homesteads, cabins and mining claims.

Purple nightshade (Solanum xantii). This is a perennial up to three feet high. Oval leaves are lobed at the base and are dark green. Umbrella-like flowers are bright purple with yellow centers. This species is found in Coastal Sage Scrub and Chaparral, especially along roads and other openings in the habitat.

Yellow/White

California bush sunflower (Encelia californica). This bush grows up to five feet tall. It has green leaves with three veins and a long stem. Ray flowers are yellow and resemble petals. Disk flowers are brown and make up the center of the sunflower. This plant is found in Coastal Sage Scrub and sometimes Chaparral throughout the range.

California yarrow (Achillea millefolium). Green foliage is lanceolate and dissected with spines on the tips of each segment. Yarrow has alternate leafing along a one- to three-foot stalk that supports large clusters of small white flowers and a distinct smell.

Chaparral morning glory (Calystegia macrostegia). This is a common twining perennial in Chaparral. Its leaves are arrowhead shaped and no longer than two inches. Its funnel-shaped flowers are pink, white or cream colored. Introduced species of morning glory can be invasive; however, this species is limited in its spread.

Common fiddleneck (Amsinckia intermedia). The common fiddleneck is twenty-four to thirty inches high. Its green linear leaves grow to about six inches and are longest near the base. Flowers are yellow to light orange and grow in curling clusters at the end of stems.

Field mustard (Brassica rapa). This is a common weed introduced from Europe probably as early as mission times. Leaves are lanceolate to oblong and not more than three inches. Showy yellow flowers with a distinct mustard smell often turn entire slopes into beautiful yellow scenes now synonymous with Southern California. Plants can grow as high as thirty-six inches.

Gold fields (Lasthenia chrysostoma). Gold fields are low-growing herbs branching from the base. The plant has small bright yellow flowers. Its leaves are one inch long and very narrow. It can be found in Valley Grassland, Vernal Pool and Coastal Sage Scrub, where this species covers large areas like 1970s shag carpet.

Prickly poppies often line roads and trails.

Jimson weed, sacred datura (Datura meteloides). Jimson weed is a dark green to gray-green perennial herb. Its leaves are one and a half to five inches long, often emitting a foul scent when disturbed. It has large white to violet cone-shaped flowers. This species is know to have psychedelic properties and was used in religious ceremonies by local native people. It can be extremely dangerous and even deadly if misused.

Matillaja poppy (Romneya coulterii). This sometimes-large bush produces the most spectacular fried egg–like flower four to eight inches across. The flowers have bright white petals with yellow centers. Plants spread from root suckers. It is difficult to cultivate outside of the wild. This plant often puts on spectacular displays on hillsides throughout the range.

Prickly pear, coastal cholla (Opuntia species). We commonly call four species from the genus *Opuntia* prickly pear. The only other member of that genus is the slightly rarer cholla cactus. Prickly pear have green paddle-shaped stems resembling a beaver's tail, which is another name for some species from this genus. Cholla have similar colored stems, but instead of paddle-shaped stems, the cholla's stems are cylindrical. Both varieties from the genus *Opuntia* are often found in large, impenetrable thickets. Bright red fruits are edible and especially sweet on the prickly pear. Be careful, however, because both the stems and fruits are well armed with stiff, sharp spines. Flowers are yellow, red and sometimes white.

Prickly poppy (Argemone munita). *Arrgemone munita robusta* is endemic to the Santa Ana Mountains. These herbaceous plants are prickly on their stems.

Their flowers are large and have yellow centers. At a distance, they may be mistaken for Matillaja poppies, described earlier.

Seep spring monkeyflower (Mimulus guttatus). This perennial has oval leaves and bright yellow flowers, usually with red spots. It is common in wet places like springs and stream banks.

Spanish bayonet (Yucca whipplei). This plant has many one-and-a-half- to two-foot stiff, sharp and pointed leaves protruding from a single base. Its cream-colored flowers grow on a long stock five to fifteen feet high. Stalks stand for some time after the flowers dry out. Pollinated by yucca moths, Spanish bayonet is found in Coastal Sage Scrub, Chaparral and along Riparian Woodland edges. This plant was used for fiber and eaten by local native people.

RED/ORANGE

California poppy (Eschscholzia californica). This is the official flower of the state of California. Petals are usually bright orange but may be yellow or even red on occasion. Leaves are dissected and spread from the base. This plant is common in grassy and open areas in most habitats; it sometimes covers large areas in a golden-orange carpet.

Fringed Indian pink (Silene lacinata). A hairy, many-stemmed plant up to eighteen inches tall. Its five petals are deeply sliced and may appear as many; the flowers are bright red. Its leaves are opposite, linear to lanceolate and sticky. Fringed Indian pink is common in Coastal Sage Scrub and Chaparral.

Humboldt lily (Lilium humboldtii). This plant has bright green leaves in four to five whorls spaced evenly along stems up to twelve feet high. Its flowers are orange with maroon spots and very showy. It can be found along Riparian corridors and is often mistakenly called a tiger lily.

Indian paintbrush (Castillaja species). At least four species of Indian paintbrush are know to occur in the Santa Ana Mountains. The plants usually have single stalks, rarely branching. Leaves grow directly from the stalk and are green, except near the top, where they are bright red and often mistaken for flowers. The flowers are also found near the top and are greenish and tubular shaped.

Fringed Indian pink. *Photo by Joel Robinson.*

Scarlet monkeyflower (Mimulus cardinalis). This plant's flowers are usually bright red but occasionally yellowish orange and have two distinct lips. This much-branching perennial with oblong, three- to five-veined leaves is found on cliffs and terraces in shaded, moist canyons.

Shrubs

The Santa Ana Mountains are a landscape of shrubs, an elfin forest rich in life. One cannot know the range without first getting to know the shrubs that blanket most of its slopes. Some of the shrubs that grow in the Santa Ana Mountains are common from Baja north to San Francisco or even Oregon. Others are strictly Southern Californian.

The next several pages contain descriptions of twenty-five shrubs one is likely to encounter or that should be sought out while visiting the Santa Ana Mountains. They are listed according to their family, but not all families are represented.

ANACARDIACEAE

Laurel sumac (Alosma laurina). An abundant evergreen shrub six to twelve feet high with smooth reddish brown bark. Its thick and leathery leaves, two to four inches long, are simple and oblong or ovate. Tiny white flowers are found in clusters at the end of branches. People with sensitive skin may develop a rash when making contact with this bush, though it is rare.

Lemonade berry (Rhus integrifolia). This shrub is common in the north part of the range below 2,500 feet. It is ten to twelve feet high with simple, ovate to elliptical leaves, occasionally with one or two lateral lobes near the base. The leaves are dark green above and lighter, with raised veins, below. Lemonade berry has small white or pink flowers. This plant is named for a refreshing drink that can be made by soaking the berries in water.

Poison oak (Toxicodendron diversilobum). This plant has a highly variable growth structure. It can be a ground cover, shrub or vine. Leaf shape also varies greatly but always has three leaflets. It is often toothed or lobed and tends to mimic plants around it, looking more like oak when in an oak woodland or like blackberry when growing in a thicket of berries. All parts of the plant secrete oil, which causes a rash on most people. Colors of leaves vary seasonally—red and falling off in fall and green from winter through summer. Poison oak is found in all habitats below five thousand feet but is most common along streams.

Poison oak can be found throughout the range, especially along creeks and canyon bottoms.

Sugarbush (Rhus ovate). Sugarbush is common throughout the range, erect or spreading with deep burgundy bark that becomes rough with age. Leaves are oval or elliptical and fold inward along the mid-rib; they are shiny on both sides. Flowers are white or pink, and the plant's red quarter-inch fruit are covered in a wax coating.

ASTERACEAE

Coast sagebrush (Artemisia californica). This grayish green shrub grows to five feet in height, with leaves that are parted once or twice into linear sections less than a millimeter wide. It is an aromatic relative of Great Basin sagebrush. Coast sagebrush is also known as California sagebrush and is an important member of the Coastal Sage Scrub community.

CAPRIFOLIACEAE

Snowberry (Symphoricarpus mollis). Snowberry is a low-spreading shrub. Its olive-green leaves are oval or round and deciduous, sometimes lobed or toothed slightly. It has pink flowers in small clusters and can be found on shaded slopes in Riparian Woodlands.

ERICACEAE

Manzanita (Arctostaphylos spp). The two species of manzanita one is likely to encounter in the Santa Ana Mountains are Eastwood manzanita and big-berry manzanita. These attractive shrubs are found above one thousand feet but are most abundant above three thousand feet in elevation. Manzanitas are evergreen, with leaves that are a dull light green. Branches spread from a burl at the base. Bark is very smooth and red, sometimes peeling. Lateral sections of limbs will die and turn woody brown while living tissue remains red. Manzanita berries are an important food source for wildlife and make a refreshing drink for humans.

FAGACEAE

Scrub oak (Quercus berberidifolia). This oak very rarely grows taller than fifteen feet. Leaves vary in shape but are usually toothed and spiny; they are dark green above and gray-green beneath. This little oak is a dominant member of most Chaparral communities and is probably the most common shrub oak in California.

Black sage (Salvia mellifera). This shrub is usually three to six feet high. Its dark green leaves are elongated and several inches long, and its pale blue or violet flowers grow in whorls. Black sage gets its name from the dark color of its branches when mature. It is an important member of the Coastal Sage Scrub community and has recently become an important agricultural plant because as bees collect its pollen they make a tasty honey available only from California apiaries.

Chia sage (Salvia columbariae). This small plant is hardly a shrub but is closely related to the other *Salvia*, so it seemed appropriate to include it here. It has dull green leaves that appear to be folded or wrinkled and are one to three inches long. Leaf margins are toothed or lobed. Small blue or purple flowers are whorled along square stems. Spiny bracts below the flowers are maroon. This plant's seeds are high in protein and provide energy when eaten. They were a staple food for many indigenous cultures, often carried by people as they walked trails. To this day, chia sage can be found growing along the oldest trails in the range. I like to believe that they were planted accidentally as seeds dropped from a buckskin pouch as a hurried but agile Acjachemen scout ran along the trail.

Purple sage (Salvia leucophylla). This strong-smelling shrub has leaves that are lighter green than those of black sage but not as gray as those of white sage. Its leaves are elongated and not more than three inches long. Blooms are bright purple and in whorls at the end of branches. Purple sage reaches its southern limit in the Santa Ana Mountains.

White sage (Salvia apiana). This showy shrub grows up to six feet high. Bits branches are white, and leaves are gray-green and whorled on the branches. The leaves are lance shaped and two to four inches long. White sage is very aromatic and often used as incense. A sacred herb to local native people and one with significant medicinal properties, this plant is an important member of the Coastal Sage Scrub community.

California bay (Umbellularia californica). This is a full tree in many northern forests, but in the Santa Ana Mountains it rarely grows to twenty feet. This aromatic tree has simple, alternate and oblong leaves three to five inches long. California bays grow in draws and on slopes below four thousand feet. Its leaves can be used in cooking but are stronger than those of the European species. More than one local chef has suggested that half as much California bay gets you more than enough spice.

POLYGONACEAE

California buckwheat (Eriogonum fasciculatum). This common erect shrub grows to three feet high. Leaves are evergreen and less than one inch long, tapering at each end. Leaves grow in clusters directly from branches. Flowers are pinkish white and in popcorn-like clusters that turn brown by mid-summer. California buckwheat is an important member of the Coastal Sage Scrub community. It is a great bee plant.

RHAMNACEAE

Buck brush (Ceonothus crassifolius). Buck brush is a common shrub in low-elevation Chaparral and Coastal Sage Scrub. It has grayish brown to white branches and thick, leathery leaves that are olive green on top and white and whorly beneath. Its flowers are small and white.

Coffeeberry (Rhamnus californica). This rounded shrub can grow up to twelve feet. Leaves are variable but usually are lanceolate with tiny teeth. The drier the habitat, the thicker the leaves. Young limbs are reddish brown; flowers are small and greenish. Its berries range from red to black. Coffeeberry is found below 3,500 feet.

Wild California lilac (Ceonothus leucadermis). This evergreen shrub has stiff and pointed branchlets, smooth light green bark and elliptical to ovate leaves rounded at its base. Its white or blue flowers are clustered on leafless branches.

ROSACEAE

California wild rosa (Rosa californica). This plant shrubs up to nine feet high. It is thorny with odd pinnate leaves. Its flowers are rosy-pink or white and much smaller than most ornamental roses. It can be found in moist places like canyon bottoms. Early Spanish explorers wrote about the scent of roses that filled the air as they approached Santiago Creek and the Santa Ana River.

Chamise (Adenostoma fasciculatum). This shrub can grow up to twelve feet. It has straight and narrow branches with protruding clusters of leaves one-quarter to one-half inch long, straight and pointed. Sometimes the leaves are divided into two or more lobes. Chamise stands are often dense and impenetrable to hikers. This species probably covers more area than any other single plant in the range.

Mountain mahogany (Cercocarpus species). Six species of *Cercocarpus* are native to California; two of these are found in the Sierra de Santa Ana. *C. betuloides* and *C. minutiflorus* are common throughout the range in Chaparral communities. These are evergreen or drought deciduous with simple, alternate leaves and small, petal-less flowers. Native people used the bark of these species to make dye.

Toyon (Heteromeles arbutifolia). This evergreen shrub has simple, alternate, two- to four-inch-long leaves, three-quarters to one and a half inches wide. The leaves are oblong, toothed and dark green on top and lighter below. It has small white flowers and berry-like fruit and is also known as Christmas berry and false holly. This species is the namesake of Hollywood. I find it ironic that Hollywood was named for something it isn't. The berries bloom in winter, making this plant a popular holiday decorating choice.

SAXIFRAGACEAE

Gooseberries and currants (Ribes spp.). These are common shrubs of which six species are found on the slopes of the Santa Ana Mountains. Some species have spines. The leaves are simple, alternate and palmately lobed. Flowers are usually in groups but can, in some cases, be solitary. The fruit is a berry.

Sticky monkeyflower (Mimulus puniceus). This plant is a freely branched erect shrub. Its leaves are two inches long and lance shaped, dark green on top, lighter below and sticky. Its flowers are various shades of orange to yellow and two inches long. Sticky monkeyflower is common below 2,500 feet.

Trees

"Few are altogether deaf to the preaching of pine trees," wrote John Muir. "Their sermons on the mountains go to our hearts; and if people in general could be got into the woods, even for once, to hear the trees

Fuchsia-flowered gooseberry is attractive in bloom.

speak for themselves, all the difficulties in the way of forest preservation would vanish."

The next several pages are dedicated to the trees found in the Santa Ana Mountains. Centuries-old oak woodlands can be found throughout the range, and many noteworthy conifer stands are located here as well. So go to the mountains and listen to the trees; they have much to teach.

CONIFERS

Big-cone Douglas fir (Pseudotsuga macrocarpa). This is a distinctive conifer that grows up to sixty feet high. Its branches are slightly upturned at the ends. Its crown comes to a point at the top. Six-inch cones distinguish this tree from the common Douglas fir, which has cones less than half that size. One-and-a-half-inch needles are blue green and flat. One of the largest-known stands of this species occurs in Trabuco Canyon.

Coulter pine (Pinus coulteri). This is the largest of the conifers in the Santa Ana Mountains. It grows up to eighty feet high with a broad and pointed crown. Bark is dark brown. Its needles are in groups of three and six to twelve inches long and blue green. This tree is abundant along the crest of the range. The cones of the Coulter pine are the heaviest known. Some are eighteen inches long and may weigh up to ten pounds. Seeds from these cones were an important food source for native peoples. Extra precipitation from summer fogs may explain the dense stands of this tree along the crest.

Knobcone pine (Pinus attenuate). This pine tree grows twenty to thirty feet tall, often with a forked trunk. Its needles are in groups of three; they are about four inches long and yellowish-green. Its cones are uniquely curved, with knobs on the outside edge only. This pine is restricted to serpentine soil. The Santa Ana Mountains' population is the southernmost in California.

Top: Coulter pine cones are known as widow makers because of their large size.

Right: Knobcone pines grow on serpentine soil in the Santa Ana Mountains.

Monterey pine (Pinus radiate). This medium-sized pine was introduced to the range and can be found growing in several stands near the crest. It can grow to nearly one hundred feet; however, it generally is closer to fifty feet in the Santa Ana Mountains. Its medium-length needles grow in clusters of three. Its cones are approximately six inches in length.

Tecate cypress (Cupressus guadalupensis). This rare tree grows in acidic soil that discourages chaparral. Its reddish-brown bark is usually smooth but is sometimes peeling off, and its leaves are scaled needles. This species is closely associated with fires, as its cones require extreme heat to open and release seeds. The largest and oldest of this species are believed to occur in the Santa Ana Mountains.

BROADLEAVED FLOWERING TREES

Big-leaf maple (Acer macrophyllum). This is a medium-sized tree with typical three- to five-lobed maple leaves sixteen to twenty-four inches long. Its flowers come in drooping clusters. The big-leaf maple is found in deep, moist canyons along streams. Though the quantity is limited, sap of these trees has been used to make maple syrup.

California walnut (Juglans californica). This deciduous tree is native to coastal Southern California. It can grow up to thirty feet high, usually with a forked trunk. Its leaves are up to nine inches long with seven or more leaflets. This walnut produces small but tasty nuts. It is found in fertile soil below three thousand feet and usually in Riparian Woodlands or just above.

Canyon oak (Quercus chrysolepis). This is the most widely distributed oak in California. Its growth form varies with environmental conditions—it can be tall with single trunks or wide spreading with multiple trunks. Its leaves are two to three inches long, elliptical, dark green above and blue gray below. Leaf margins can be smooth or spiny. Canyon oak bark is scab-like and often covered with lichens.

Coast live oak (Quercus agrifolia). The coast live oak is an evergreen oak, usually wider than it is tall and almost always with crooked and spreading limbs. Its leaves are dark green above and lighter beneath, and they curve under. Usually, the leaves are spiny, but to what degree varies greatly. Some ecologists, including myself, believe that it depends on how much the tree

Coast live oaks are the most common tree oak in the Santa Ana Mountains.

has been browsed by deer and other animals, as the lower leaves tend to be more deeply toothed than those on upper limbs above the browse line. Coast live oak is found in valleys and on less arid slopes.

Engelmann oak (Quercus engelmannii). This is a medium-sized drought deciduous oak with rounded or elliptical canopies. Its trunk is light gray or white and up to fourteen feet in diameter. Leaves are usually one to three inches long, blue green and flat or wavy with toothless margins. Engelmann oaks are found above the coastal plain and below 4,500 feet. They were once widely distributed throughout Southern California but are now limited to a few small stands and scattered individuals. The largest preserved stand is on the Santa Rosa Plateau on the eastern slopes of the range.

Flowering ash (Fraxinus dipetala). This small tree has two-petaled white flowers in drooping clusters. Its leaves are six inches long with three to seven toothed leaflets. Flowering ash is common on the upper edges of Riparian Woodlands. Velvet ash is also found there but is less common.

Oak woodland.

Fremont's cottonwood (Populus fremontii). Fremont's cottonwoods are common throughout the Southwest United States. They are often large trees that top sixty feet in some places. In the Santa Ana Mountains, however, these trees rarely top forty feet. Leaves are triangular to heart shaped, two to five inches and finely toothed. Mature cottonwoods have deeply furrowed bark. This is an important member of the Riparian Woodlands of Southern California.

Interior live-oak (Quercus wislizenii). This is a rounded, full-canopied tree. The elliptical leaves can be spiny or with smooth margins. Unlike the coast live oak, the leaves of this species are flat. Its leaves are dark green above and lighter beneath. Younger trees have gray bark becoming darker with age. They are common in Chaparral above 2,700 feet elevation.

Pacific madrone (Arbutus menziesii). These trees are twenty-five to eighty feet high, common in the Northwest but rare in Southern California. Their leaves are four to six inches long and up to three inches wide. Leaf margins are smooth or with very tiny teeth. The bark is smooth, red or yellowish and sometimes peeling. Pacific madrone resembles extremely large manzanitas. The Trabuco Canyon population is the southernmost known occurrence of this attractive tree.

Red willow (Salix laevigata). This is the most common willow in the range. It grows to forty feet but is most commonly in the ten- to twenty-foot size range in the Santa Ana Mountains. It has rough reddish-brown bark, and its leaves are lance shaped and light green above, lighter below. Its catkins are one to three inches long. The red willow is found along drainages below five thousand feet.

White alder (Alnus rhombifolia). The oval leaves of this tree have small teeth along their margins. About a dozen small veins spread from the large mid-vein. Alders grow along streams in canyon bottoms. White alder has become quite popular with the locals for the good-quality walking sticks that wash out of the canyons every winter.

CREEPING, CRAWLING CRITTERS AND FISH

Bugs are probably the least favorite of the critters encountered in the Santa Ana Mountains, though amphibians and reptiles play a very close second. Nobody likes to find a black widow spider under his sleeping bag or a toe biter beetle frolicking in his favorite swimming hole. And even children's stories call out the frog when the fairy princess faints or gags prior to having to kiss him to find her prince. Nobody wants to kiss a frog, and our dislike for the snake goes back to biblical roots. Whatever the season, wherever the habitat, creeping, crawling and flying bugs and other critters are bound to be there.

In fact, bugs (insects, arachnids and their relatives) make up nearly 80 percent of the animal kingdom. For those who take the time to get past the unique and sometimes unattractive appearance of bugs, exciting discoveries await. Because they are so numerous and diverse, I will attempt to describe only the more commonly encountered and interesting here. For more detailed and complete listings, an insect guide is recommended.

Water Bugs

Many insects are associated with water, as a quick look into any pool in the range would demonstrate. A common misconception is that the presence of these critters means the water is dirty or polluted, but this simply isn't true. Following are descriptions of a few of the water bugs found in the Santa Ana Mountains.

Common blue darner dragonfly. Although found in water only at the earliest stages of their lives, dragonflies are commonly seen along streams and near other water sources. This one is royal blue and an inch to an inch and a half in size. It is a fast, darting dragonfly found near streams feeding on mosquitoes.

Common red skimmer dragonfly. Reddish orange and two to three and a half inches long, this dragonfly is found along streams and canyon bottoms. It feeds on mosquitoes and other insects and is the most common dragonfly in the range.

Toe biter. This infrequently seen large aquatic insect has an oval body of varying shades of brown and powerful front legs. It feeds on other insects, small fish and snakes and has been known to bite people, causing a stinging sensation and swelling. It is a voracious predator.

Water strider. This is one of the most common water insects in the region. It skis across the water on four long, slender legs and uses its two short front legs for catching and holding prey. It has a long, narrow body. The unique shadow of this insect is often seen jetting across the floor of small pools before the actual insect is spotted gliding across the surface of the water.

Whirligig beetle. This is a small, dark carnivorous beetle. It buzzes around the water like a wind-up toy. It has two pairs of eyes, one used above the surface of the water and one used below. I once watched a half dozen whirligig beetles devour a large grasshopper. The vigor with which they tore at the still-struggling prey rivaled that of lions and wolves.

Social Insects

Ants, bees and wasps are among the social insects found in the Santa Ana Mountains. Some of the ants in the region have even taken to a pastoral lifestyle, raising "herds" of aphids. The ants that feed on the fluid produced by the aphids move their herds from plant to plant, ensuring a steady food supply for the aphids and themselves.

Bees appear to be more common in the range today than they were one hundred years ago because beekeeping was a popular livelihood among early settlers. Honeybees have become naturalized in the Santa Anas and find the old hollows of the many large oaks in the range to be great habitats. Although the exotic honeybee is the most recognizable bee in the range, many native species also thrive here. Don't get too close to any of the bees, though, as Africanized or "killer bees" have made homes in the area and are likely found in the Santa Ana Mountains.

Wasps, however, are the most diverse and fascinating of this insect group. Following are descriptions of the more common and interesting of these social critters.

Gall wasp. These are usually smaller wasps, and although they are not regularly seen, signs of their presence are common. These are the critters that produce the hollow wooden balls seen on oaks in the range. They prefer live oaks and insert their eggs beneath the bark of small limbs. As the eggs hatch and the larvae grow, the galls form. When the wasps reach maturity, they leave the security of the galls.

Tarantula hawk wasp. This is a large, jet-black wasp with orange wings, common in the Santa Anas. It kills and lays eggs on tarantulas and other spiders. Prey serves as a food source for young.

Velvet ant. The velvet ant is actually a wasp. Females are wingless; males have wings. Females are commonly seen crawling along the ground and appear to be large, furry ants. Females have a powerful sting; males are harmless. Velvet ants are usually red and black, but some species are white or yellow.

Moths and Butterflies

Moths and butterflies are common in the Santa Ana Mountains, and some species may even depend on this range for survival. When attempting to distinguish moths from butterflies, I recommend looking at antennae. Those of moths will be feather-like, while butterfly antennae resemble clubs. Several of the more common and interesting butterflies and moths are described below.

California dogface butterfly. This is the California state butterfly. It is sulfur green underneath, and the tops of its rear wings are bright orange. The tops of its pointed forewings are black except along the edges and on the "dogface" in the center, both of which are orange.

Harbison's dun skipper. This species resembles a moth but is a true butterfly. It is brown all over but lighter on the bottom and has very faint markings and triangular wings. It is typically one to one and a half inches and feeds on San Diego sedge. It has been recommended for protection under the Endangered Species Act. There are several scattered populations of the dun skipper in the Santa Ana Mountains.

Mourning cloak. This butterfly is dark brown or black underneath with paler edges. Its top is black with yellowish cream edges. It has purple or blue spots along the entire edge. Mourning cloak is common in the spring along Riparian corridors. Sometimes willow trees are completely defoliated by the caterpillars of this species.

Yucca moth. These are small white moths that practice a symbiotic relationship with species of yucca. The adult moths cross-pollinate the plants while laying their eggs. As seedpods develop, the eggs hatch, and the larvae feed on some of the seeds, leaving others for continued propagation of the plant. Both the moths and yuccas have been declining in numbers recently.

Beetles

Beetles are as common in the Santa Ana Mountains as they are everywhere else. In fact, there are more species of beetles than any other known organism. A few are described below.

California prionus beetle. A long-horned beetle with long antennae with serrated edges, the California prionus comes in various shades of brown and sometimes almost black. This interesting beetle looks like a miniature dinosaur or prehistoric creature. I am so enamored with this beetle that I had one tattooed on my arm. It can inflict a painful bite when threatened. Do not let one of these get ahold of you. Ouch!

Common ground beetle. This large black beetle is commonly seen crawling along trails, especially in the evening and morning. When startled, ground beetles will lower their heads and raise their hind ends in defense. These beetles are often referred to as stink bugs because of the strong-smelling fluid released when captured or threatened.

Ladybird beetle. Commonly called the ladybug, this is a small, distinct flying beetle. It can be red, orange or yellow and often has a varying number of black spots. A most beneficial critter, the ladybird eats aphids, white flies and mites. It is often seen in clumps of hundreds of thousands near peaks. When mating time arrives, individuals fly to the highest point, around which they congregate for mating.

Spiders

Spiders are abundant in the Santa Ana Mountains, as anyone who has done much hiking in the range knows. It is difficult to hike along any of the trails without breaking through invisible webs. Following are descriptions of two of the most interesting spiders in the range.

Black widow. These are large, web-building spiders. Females are jet black with a red hourglass on the bottom of their abdomens. Males are smaller and lighter in color; they also lack the red marking. These spiders weave complex webs that sometimes appear messy at first glance but show true intricacy upon closer inspection. Webs generally can be found eight to twenty-four inches off the ground and are often constructed above rodent holes, allowing spiders to hide during the day. Black widows are common in the Santa Ana Mountains—and poisonous, so beware!

Tarantula. These are large, dark and furry spiders. Mostly nocturnal, they are occasionally seen in the early morning. Four to six inches in length, they spend their days in holes near grassy open areas. They can inflict a painful bite; their front legs and mouths are very strong.

Fish

First-time visitors to the Santa Ana Mountains would probably be surprised to find out that more than a dozen species of fish can be found in the streams and reservoirs of the generally arid range. All but three of the species have been introduced, mostly for the benefit of those fishing at Irvine Lake.

Prior to the overdevelopment of the coastal plain and resulting lowered water table, many of the streams that now are intermittent once had significant flows throughout the year and supported a great deal more fish than they do today. Evidence of this is Fisherman's Camp in the San Mateo Canyon Wilderness, once a car camp for those fishing in Tenaja and San Mateo Creeks. Santiago, San Juan, San Mateo and Trabuco Creeks once supported thriving steelhead spawning runs. All were believed to have disappeared; however, spawning steelhead have been seen in Trabuco and San Mateo Creeks recently. Fisherman's Camp is still a great trail camp; however, I would not count on catching dinner in the creek any longer, as most of the fish there are still well below catchable size.

Following are brief descriptions of the native fish in the range and a list of the others found here. For those who wish to fish while visiting the Santa Anas, I recommend Irvine Lake.

Arroyo chub. This minnow is brownish green or gray and three to five inches long. Found in small streams with year-round pools and cool, clear water, this species is closely related to a chub found in Sonora, Mexico, and probably has existed in the Peninsular Ranges since they began moving north along the San Andreas Fault millions of years ago.

Santa Ana sucker. This is a very localized fish, one of eleven native suckers in California. A bottom-dwelling fish, it feeds on small organisms. It has a slightly humped back and a stout, club-shaped head. It is now becoming rare and has been given protection under the Endangered Species Act.

Steelhead (rainbow) trout. Steelhead and rainbow trout are essentially identical fish, only steelhead are anadramous, choosing, when possible, to spend part of their lives in the ocean. Their backs are a light brownish green with pink to almost red sides. Their heads and bodies are speckled. Steelhead spawn in late winter or early spring. Anywhere from six to fifteen inches, they are also known as silver trout.

Three-spine stickleback. This increasingly rare fish appears almost prehistoric. Its distinct spines on the back make its identification undeniable. Historically found in mid- and low-level coastal streams throughout the state, it is now limited to a few locations, including Santiago Creek in the Santa Ana Mountains.

The following checklist of fish in the Santa Ana Mountains was taken from *Life in the Chaparral* by Barry Thomas:

Arroyo chub (*Gila orcutii*)
Black bullhead (*Ictalurus melas*)
Bluegill (*Lepomis cyanellus*)
Brown bullhead (*Ictalurus nebulosus*)
Carp (*Cyprinus carpio*)
Channel catfish (*Ictalurus punctatus*)
Goldfish (*Carassius auratus*)
Green sunfish (*Lepomis macrochirus*)
Large-mouth bass (*Micropterus salmoides*)
Mosquito fish (*Gambusia affinis*)
Mullet (*Mugil cephalus*)
Rainbow trout (*Saslmo gairdneri*)
Santa Ana sucker (*Pantosteus santaanae*)
Three-spined stickleback (*Gasterosteus aculeatus*)

Amphibians

At least fourteen species of amphibians have been documented in the Santa Ana Mountains, and another is known to occur in the foothills. Amphibians can live in fresh water or on the land because they can absorb oxygen directly through their skin. Toads, frogs and salamanders are the three groups of amphibians found in the Santa Ana Mountains. Amphibians are important because they can be used as an indicator species for the overall health of their habitats; many are threatened with extinction.

African clawed frog. This frog, anywhere from two and a half to six inches long, is an introduced, destructive species. Formerly used in laboratory tests to determine human pregnancies, it eats anything and everything. It is smooth-skinned with a flat-looking body. Eradication is currently being attempted; however, this species is still readily available in most pet stores.

Arboreal salamander. This lung-less salamander, two to four inches long, has a noticeably large head and strong limbs. It is brownish in color with yellow spots or blotches. This species squeals when captured. Its preferred habitat is coastal live oak woodlands.

The endangered arroyo toad is found along several creeks in the range. *Photo by Joel Robinson.*

Arroyo toad. Ranging in size from two to four inches, this frog is pinkish brown to gray green. It ccupies stream terraces with moderate-sized Riparian forests. It is protected as an endangered species, which limits access to its breeding areas during spring.

Black-bellied slender salamander. At one to two inches long, this salamander resembles a worm with tiny legs. It is completely terrestrial and found in soil of a variety of habitats. Members of this species have dark bellies with white spattering and an orange-red dorsal stripe.

Bullfrog. Four to eight inches. Introduced species found in or near permanent pools. Preys on Arroyo toads and Red-legged frogs. Has few natural enemies.

California newt. Two and a half to three and a half inches long, this species is the most common in the Santa Ana Mountains, occurring up to three thousand feet in elevation. Primarily diurnal, it is terrestrial except when breeding. Rough-skinned during its terrestrial phase, it becomes smooth-skinned when aquatic. It has a bright orange ventral surface.

California newts are common in many canyons in the range.

California slender salamander. Anywhere from one and a half to three inches long, this salamander is found in moist environments, such as under logs or rocks and near streams. Like all lung-less salamanders, this one resembles a worm with tiny legs.

California tree frog. This frog is grayish brown with darker blotches and ranges in size from one to two inches. It lacks the black-eye stripe of the Pacific tree frog. It is most abundant along rocky streambeds. A good climber, it sounds like a duck.

Ensatina. At one and a half to five inches, this species is dark brown with yellowish markings around the base of its legs. Its preferred habitat is under rotting logs.

Pacific slender salamander. One and a half to three inches in length, the Pacific slender is usually light brown or pink to red. It is found in numerous habitats, including Woodlands, Chaparral and Valley Grassland.

99

Pacific tree frogs are the most common frogs in the Santa Ana Mountains.

Pacific tree frog. At one to two inches, this is the most abundant frog in the range. Found at all elevations, it can change its shade of color rapidly. It has a distinct black-eye stripe that does not change color. Adhesive toe pads make members of this species excellent climbers.

Red-legged frog. This large (one and a half to six inches), completely aquatic frog is yellowish in color with a red lower body and undersides of its legs. Found in deep pools with overhung, densely vegetated banks, it is near extinction in the Santa Ana Mountains due to a lowered water table and loss of habitat.

Tiger salamander. From three to six and a half inches long, the tiger salamander is dark brown with yellowish tiger-like stripes. It is the only salamander population at Irvine Lake, where it was introduced by fisherman who use it for bait.

Western spadefoot toad. At one and a half to three inches, this is not a true toad! It can be identified by a sharp "spade" on its hind legs and vertical pupils. Its spade feet are used to burrow deep into ground, where it remains until the rainy season. The spadefoot breeds in temporary pools; it can metamorphose in a few days.

Western toad. Anywhere from two to six inches, this wart-covered toad has a single whitish yellow stripe down the center of its back. Found in a variety of habitats, including Valley Grassland and Woodlands, it is mainly nocturnal, hiding in rodent burrows during the day. It gathers at pools during winter for mating. Chirping vocalizations.

Reptiles

More than thirty species of reptiles have been identified in the Santa Ana Mountains. Many are rarely seen, while other are hard to miss. Some can be dangerous, but most are harmless or even beneficial. Following are descriptions of some of the more common, interesting or endangered reptiles found in the Santa Ana Mountains. Because not all reptiles present in the Santa Anas are described, a checklist has been included for the reader's benefit.

California king snake. This common snake is the friendliest of the local snakes because it is generally calm and easy to handle. In addition, it commonly preys on rattlesnakes. The brown or sometimes black snake has beige, off-white or yellow stripes crossing its body. Rarely, the lighter stripe runs the length of the body.

California legless lizard. This lizard has no legs but differs from a snake because it has movable eyelids and external ear openings. It burrows in loose sand or under organic litter and is found in woodlands and canyon bottoms.

California (San Diego) mountain king snake. The mountain king has red, black and beige bands from head to tail. It resembles a coral snake but is not dangerous. It is also known to prey on rattlesnakes.

Coachwhip. This is a fast, slim, diurnal snake. It is grayish pink with black crossbars on its neck. It is a good climber. Coachwhips bite but are not venomous.

Coast horned lizard. Known to most as the horny toad, this critter is actually a true lizard. It has a flat, broad body with spikes behind its head and a sharp scale along its back. It can be found in Coastal Sage Scrub, Chaparral and Grasslands communities.

Gopher snakes are known to mimic rattlesnakes but lack the rattle and venom of their cousins.

Gopher snake. This large, strong snake is beige with dark reddish brown spots or square markings along its back. It mimics rattlesnakes by coiling and shaking its tail. It is found in Grasslands, Woodlands and Chaparral communities.

Granite spiny lizard. The male granite spiny has a yellow or green dorsal surface with a purple stripe on its back. It eats flowers and leaves, as well as insects. It can be found in Oak Woodlands and Chaparral communities.

Orange-throated whiptail. With its bright orange throat and striped sides, this species is at the northern limit of its range in the Santa Ana Mountains. Once considered to be rare and given protection under the Endangered Species Act, this lizard can still be seen more often than one might think. It prefers the Coastal Sage Scrub habitat.

Red-diamond rattlesnake. This large, reddish brown snake with rough diamond markings along its back is the least aggressive of the rattlesnakes found in the Santa Ana Mountains. It is found in Coastal Sage Scrub and Chaparral communities.

Rosy boa. Grayish red with three brown stripes and smooth skin, the rosy boa suffocates its prey by constriction. It is nocturnal and active in below-freezing temperatures.

Southern alligator lizard. The southern alligator has a long, slim body with short limbs. A groove or slit is present along its side and is often infested with tiny ticks. The bites of this lizard can be painful but are not poisonous.

Speckled rattlesnake. Found almost exclusively in rocky habitats, this snake's colors vary from light to dark depending on the rocks in which it is dwelling. Speckled rattlesnakes can be very aggressive.

Striped racer. Similar to the coachwhip described above but distinguished by pale stripes on each side, this snake is diurnal and fast. It is found in Chaparral communities.

Two-striped garter snake. Grayish tan or black in color with reddish spots becoming less apparent toward the tail, the two-striped garter is strictly aquatic. It feeds on tadpoles, including those from genus *Bufo*, which are toxic to most predators.

Western banded gecko. This nocturnal species has smooth skin and is light colored with dark stripes and spots. It squeaks when captured and can be found in Chaparral communities.

Banded geckos are attractive but rare.

Western pond turtles were once common throughout Southern California but now are limited to a few canyons and creeks. *Photo by Joel Robinson.*

Western fence lizard. With large, coarse scales, a blue-green throat and sides of belly and orange under legs, this is probably the most common lizard in the range and region. It can be found in all habitats.

Western pond turtle. The only native turtle in the Santa Ana Mountains, this species used to be common but collecting and introduced predators have drastically reduced its population. It can still be found in some canyons with permanent water.

Western rattlesnake. One of the most common snakes in the range, the western rattlesnake is dark colored, sometimes black, and its markings vary. It is found in Chaparral communities.

Snakes, like other wildlife, can be dangerous when challenged. All rattlesnakes are venomous and can be deadly, but if given the chance, they will most often leave people alone.

THE BIRDS

The Santa Ana Mountains' diversity of habitats and key location on the Pacific Flyway make the range a birdwatchers' paradise. More than two hundred species of feathered friends have been recorded here, with every season providing something special to see.

If you see a bird that is not on the accompanying list, take notes and report it your local chapter of the National Audubon Society. Remember, the more detailed your notes are, the more likely your sighting is to be accepted. Ornithology, like no other science, has progressed greatly from the work of amateurs and hobbyists, so don't discount your personal observations.

When attempting to identify birds, certain general characteristics should be looked for. First, look at the size of the bird. Is it sparrow size, robin size or raven size? Simple associations like this will help locate the proper section in a field guide. Then look at coloration. What colors are the crown, breast, rump and wings? This will help narrow down the species, probably to just a few choices. If you still can't identify it, look at more specific characteristics. What shape is the

Tucker Wild Bird Sanctuary.

bird's bill? How long and what shape is its tail? By this point, you should be able to identify it, but if not, write down all the field marks, habitat descriptions and other notes and call your local birding group when you get home. In most cases, the group will be happy to help you figure it out.

Bring binoculars whenever you go to the Santa Anas, as you never what you might see. However, for those who wish to visit the range specifically to watch birds, I recommend the following places: Any canyon in the range will be rich in bird life, and the deeper the better. Modjeska Canyon is particularly good for beginners because Tucker Wild Bird Sanctuary has interpretive signs, and naturalists to help with identification. Irvine Lake is probably the best place for water birds and shorebirds, as it is the largest body of water in the range. There is an entrance fee, and boats can be rented by those who wish to go on to the lake.

Although not technically in the mountains, Lake Elsinore is absolutely tied geologically to the Santa Anas and offers miles of shoreline and many acres of Riparian Woodland. There are several areas on each side of Lake Elsinore that can be reached on foot and without paying a fee.

All of the regional parks in and around the Santa Ana Mountains offer a variety of habitats, and most have information on resident birds. The Santa Rosa Plateau is an excellent choice for birds, especially raptors. (I once encountered seven raptor species in a single afternoon!)

The Santa Ana Mountains provide a crucial habitat for many sensitive, threatened or endangered birds. "Threatened" and "Endangered" are titles given to those plants and animals that are considered likely to disappear entirely or from a significant portion of their geographic range and thus need protection under the Endangered Species Act. Some of the "T" and "E" species that might be spotted in the range include: Swainson's hawk, peregrine falcon, California least tern, least Bell's vireo and the California gnatcatcher. Other species being considered for protection include mountain quail, horned larks, cactus wrens, loggerhead shrike, rufous-crowned sparrow and tri-colored blackbird.

The United States Forest Service has given "Special Interest" status to yellow warblers and golden eagles. Both of these can be found in parts of the range, although neither is commonly seen.

Year-round residents are numerous and represent a good portion of the total list of recorded species; however, each season has its surprises. Incidentals in the Santa Ana Mountains are also numerous, with Santiago Peak and areas along the Santa Ana River repeatedly producing rare sightings.

Winter is ideal for water birds and shorebirds. Irvine Lake, on occasion, hosts common loons, Canada geese, least terns and long-billed dowitchers.

Merlins are sighted every winter, as are saw-whet-owls. Mountain bluebirds and purple finches can sometimes be found in woodlands during the middle of the season. Because the climate in Southern California is so moderate, the Santa Ana Mountains serve as a refuge for many birds fleeing harsh winter conditions.

Spring is a colorful season in the Santa Ana Mountains. Yellow-bellied and red-breasted sapsuckers, violet green swallows, yellow warblers and Lazuli buntings can be found in the range at this time. Tucker Wild Bird Sanctuary in Modjeska Canyon is a nice

An Anna's hummingbird is seen with babies.

birding stop in any season, but it is especially nice in the spring. For the more adventurous, a trip to the floor of San Mateo Canyon can provide glimpses of Costa's hummingbird, least Bell's vireo and yellow-breasted chat.

Summer is the dormant season in the Santa Ana Mountains, but the birds remain active and visible in all but the hottest hours. Summer is the season to see yellow warblers, lesser nighthawks, hooded orioles and phainopeplas. Temperatures can top one hundred degrees from June through September, so bring plenty of water.

Fall is even drier than summer in the Santa Ana Mountains. Hot air rising from the desert often gusts toward the ocean at more than sixty miles per hour, drying out vegetation and creating dangerous (to humans) fire conditions. The fires of 1993 destroyed numerous structures within the range. Because of the seasonal weather conditions, raptors are a fall specialty as well. As thermals lift off the desert floor, they carry red-tail hawks, golden eagles and turkey vultures soaring high above the peaks. White-throated swifts and common ravens are also known for playing in the fall winds.

More than half the birds recorded in the Santa Anas are full-time residents. The residents, seasonal visitors and incidentals are listed at the end of the bird list provided at the end of this book.

BIRDS OF THE SANTA ANA MOUNTAINS

Loons (family Gavidae): common loon (Wu)

Grebes (family Podicipedae): eared grebe (Ru), western grebe (Ru), Clark's grebe (Rr), pied-billed grebe (Ru)

Pelican (family Pelecanidae): American white pelican (FSr)

Cormorants (family Phalacrocoracidae): double-crested cormorant (Ru)

Herons (family Ardeidae): least bittern (Sur), American bittern (Ru), black-crowned night heron (Rc), green-backed heron (FWSu), cattle egret (Ru), snowy egret (FWSc), great egret (FWSu), great blue heron (Rc)

CHECKLIST KEY TO THE BIRDS OF THE SANTA ANA MOUNTAINS

KEY TO SEASONS PRESENT
F=fall
W=winter
S=spring
Su=summer
R=resident, or present all year
M=migrant, or just stopping by

KEY TO RELATIVE ABUNDANCE
c=common, or at least common at one location
u=uncommon, present in small numbers
r=rare; very few but seen every year
i=incidental, or only a few records

Geese and ducks (family Anatidae): Canada goose (FWSr), mallard (Rc), gadwall (FWSu), green-winged teal (FWSu), American wigeon (FWSu), northern pintail (FWSu), northern shoveler (FWSu), cinnamon teal (Ru), ruddy duck (Ru), ring-necked duck (FSr), lesser scaup (Wr), common goldeneye (Wr), bufflehead (FWSu), common merganser (Wr)

Coots (family Rallidae): American coot (Rc)

Plovers (family Charadriidae): killdeer (Rc)

Sandpipers (family Scolopacidae): willet (Ru), greater yellowlegs (FWSu), lesser yellowlegs (FWSu), spotted sandpiper (FWSu), long-billed

Above: A mallard is a fairly common sight near water in the Santa Ana Mountains.

Right: Egret.

dowitcher (FWSu), common snipe (FWSu), western sandpiper (FWSc), least sandpiper (FWSc)

Gulls and terns (family Laridae): Bonaparte's gull (FWSu), ring-billed gull (Rc), herring gull (FWSr), California gull (FWSu), western gull (Ru), least tern (WSu), Caspian tern (Ru)

Vultures (family Cathartidae): turkey vulture (Rc)

Kites, hawks and eagles (family Accipitridae): golden eagle (Rr), bald eagle (Mr), black-shouldered kite (Ru), northern harrier (Rr), sharp-shinned hawk (Ru),

Cooper's hawk (Rc), red-shouldered hawk (Rc), red-tailed hawk (Rc), Swainson's hawk (Wr), rough-legged hawk (Mr), ferrugfinous hawk (Mr)

Falcons (family Falconidae): American kestrel (Rc), merlin (Wu), prairie falcon (Rr), peregrine falcon (Mi)

Quail (family Phasianidae): California quail (Rc), mountain quail (Ru), ring-necked pheasant (Ru)

Doves and pigeons (family Columbidae): band-tailed pigeon (Rc), mourning dove (Rc), spotted dove (Ru), common ground dove (Mc), rock dove (Rc)

Roadrunners (family Cuclidae): greater roadrunner (Ru)

Owls (family Tytonidae and Strigidae): barn owl (Ru), western screech owl (Rr), long-eared owl (Rr), short-eared owl (Wu), great horned owl (Rc), burrowing owl (Rr), northern saw-whet owl (Wr), California spotted owl (Rr)

Nightjars (family Caprimulgidae): common poorwill (Sr), common nighthawk (Mr), lesser nighthawk (Su)

Swifts (family Apodidae): black swift (Mr), white-throated swift (Su), Vaux's swift (Mr)

Hummingbirds (family Trochilidae): Anna's hummingbird (Rc), Allen's hummingbird (Mu), Costa's hummingbird (Sc), black-chinned hummingbird (Sc), rufous hummingbird (Mu), calliope hummingbird (Mr)

Kingfishers (family Alcedinidae): belted kingfisher (Ru)

Woodpeckers (family Picidae): northern flicker (Rc), acorn woodpecker (Rc), Lewis's woodpecker (Wr), yellow-bellied sapsucker (Sr), red-breasted sapsucker (Sr), downy woodpecker (Rr), Nuttall's woodpecker (Rc), hairy woodpecker (Wr)

Tyrant flycatchers (family Tyrannidae): western kingbird (Sc), Cassin's kingbird (Sr), ash-throated flycatcher (Sc), black Phoebe (Rc), Say's Phoebe (Ru), Pacific Slope flycatcher (Sc), olive-sided flycatcher (Mr), western wood peewee (Ru)

Larks (family Alaudidae): horned lark (Rc)

Swallows (family Hirundinidae): tree swallow (Mu), violet-green swallow (Sc), bank swallow (Sc), northern rough-winged swallow (Sr), barn swallow (Sr), cliff swallow (Sc), purple martin (Si)

Jays and crows (family Corvidae): scrub jay (Rc), steller's jay (Mi), American crow (Rc), common raven (Rc)

Titmice and chickadees (family Paridae): plain titmouse (Rc), mountain chickadee (Mi)

Bushtits (family Aegithalidae): bushtit (Rc)

Creeper (family Certhidae): brown creeper (Rc)

Nuthatches (family Sittidae): white-breasted nuthatch (Wc), red-breasted nuthatch (Wu)

Wrens (family Troglodytidae): house wren (Sc), Bewick's wren (Rc), cactus wren (Rr), canyon wren (Rr), rock wren (Rr), marsh wren (Rc)

Thrushes and allies (family Muscicapidae): American robin (Wc), varied thrush (Mr), hermit thrush (Wr), Swainson's thrush (Sr), western bluebird (Rc), mountain bluebird (Wr), Townsend's solitaire (Wi), ruby-crowned kinglet (Wc), blue-gray gnatcatcher (Ru), California gnatcatcher (Rr), wrentit (Rc)

Shrikes (family Laniidae): loggerhead shrike (Rr)

Mimic thrushes (family Mimidae): northern mockingbird (Rc), California thrasher (Rc)

Pipits (family Motacillidae): American pipit (Wi)

Waxwings (family Bombycillidae): cedar waxwings (Wi)

Silky flycatchers (family Ptiligonatidae): phainopepla (Suu)

Starlings (family Sturnidae): European starling (Rc)

Viroes (family Vireonidae): Hutton's vireo (Rr), Bell's vireo (Sr), solitary vireo (Sr), warbling vireo (Sr)

Warblers, sparrow and blackbirds (family Emberizidae): orange-crowned warbler (Rr), Nashville warbler (Mi), yellow warbler (Sr), yellow-rumped warbler (Rc), black-throated gray warbler (Sr), Townsend's warbler (SSur), hermit warbler (SSur), McGillivray's warbler (Mi), yellow-breasted chat (Sr), yellow-throated warbler (Rr), Wilson's warbler (Sc), black-and-white warbler (Sr), common yellowthroat (Sr), black-headed grosbeak (Sc), blue grosbeak (Si), Lazuli bunting (Sr), green-tailed towhee (Wr), spotted towhee (Rc), California towhee (Rc), grasshopper sparrow (Rc), lark sparrow (Rr), sage sparrow (Ri), rufous-crowned sparrow (Rr), dark-eyed junco (Wc), chipping sparrow (Wr), white-crowned sparrow (Wc), golden-crowned sparrow (Wc), black-chinned sparrow (Sc), fox sparrow (Wc), Harris's sparrow (Mr), Lincoln's sparrow (Mr), song sparrow (Rc), white-throated sparrow (Wu), vesper sparrow (Wu), Savannah sparrow (Ru), western meadowlark (Rc), red-winged blackbird (Rc), brewer's blackbird (Rc), tricolored blackbird (Rr), yellow-headed blackbird (Sr), hooded oriole (Sc), northern oriole (Sc), brown-headed cowbird (Rc), western tanager (Sc), summer tanager (Sr)

Weavers (family Passeridae): house sparrow (Rc)

Finches (family Fringillidae): pine siskin (Wi), American goldfinch (Rr), lesser goldfinch (Rc), Lawrence's goldfinch (Wr), purple finch (Wr), house finch (Rc)

CHARISMATIC CREATURES BIG AND SMALL

Of all the animals in the Santa Ana Mountains, the most widely recognized are the mammals. More than forty species of mammals are currently known to inhabit the range, and several others have been extirpated, including the California grizzly bear and the gray wolf. The last of the Southern California grizzly bears was killed in the Santa Ana Mountains near the top of Holy Jim Canyon in 1908.

There are at least a half dozen sites in the Santa Ana Mountains named for the bears that once roamed freely here, including Bear Springs near the junction of Holy Jim Trail and the Main Divide Road, Bear Canyon in the San Mateo Canyon Wilderness and Bear Flats off the Silverado Truck Trail.

Because the grizzly bear is such an important part of California's natural history and has played an important role in the biological and cultural history of the Santa Ana Mountains, an effort is underway to designate the entire range as the Grizzly Bear National Monument. (See the chapter on Conservation and the Future later in this book for more on the Grizzly Bear National Monument.)

Less is known about the wolves that once roamed the range. According to Orange County historian Jim Sleeper, the packs of wolves preferred the area now covered by Peters Canyon Reservoir. Since we know wolves require a great deal more territory than the few hundred acres of Peters Canyon Park, it is likely that they also spent a great deal of time in the woodlands at the heart of the range.

It was apparently near this site, early in the twentieth century, that the pack took down the last of the region's pronghorn antelope. The pronghorn would have preferred the grasslands that now are limited to the rolling hills around the eastern toll road and Santiago Canyon Road and on what is now the Great Park. The latter is scheduled for conversion to a more conventional park-like landscape—or worse yet, a rare landscape from some far-off place—furthering the demise of our most threatened local landscape: the valley grassland.

Jaguars are believed to have lurked in the deep canyons and crossed the ridges of the Santa Ana Mountains well into the nineteenth century and possibly were utilizing the range as late as the mid-twentieth century. The last one to be killed in California was taken down near Mount San Jacinto in 1860, though numerous reports of jaguars have been recorded since. Several of those reports have come from the Santa Ana Mountains, and at least one unconfirmed report dates to the late 1980s around Black Star Canyon.

Another mammal that is not currently a resident of the range but for which I have found records is the muskrat. Sleeper talks of a muskrat living in the Irvine Park pond around 1919; however, no later occurrences have been found. Elk were introduced into the Santa Anas in the 1950s, but due to lack of suitable habitat, they did not survive. I have never seen evidence of the elk herd myself, but I met a man in 1992 at the old Tenaja Campground who described having found an elk antler near Yeager Mesa in Trabuco Canyon in the early 1970s. He had been hunting in the range ever since in hopes of bringing down the last of the elk. He never got one.

The following pages contain descriptions of the more than forty mammals that continue to survive in the Santa Ana Mountains. While some species are almost never seen, others are quite common. This information will help you identify most of the mammals found in the range.

Audubon's cottontail rabbit. This rabbit has short hair, long legs and a fluffy white tail. Its ears are often darker near the tip, and it has narrow hind feet. Its preferred habitat is dense brush, but it can be found on the edge of thickets early in the evening.

Badger. Gray to yellowish brown, the badger has a black face with a white stripe between its eyes. These are large mammals with strong, sharp claws used for digging. Sharp teeth and claws are used for defense. Its only real enemies in the range are mountain lions, although coyotes have been seen stealing prey from badgers. Badgers are best known from the savannah and grassland habitats in other places, though early studies of the Santa Ana Mountains found them in Chaparral communities near road cuts.

Beaver. Beaver is rarely seen, but several colonies have become established over the last several decades. Signs are common along some waterways with year-round flows. The beaver is dark grayish brown with a flat paddle-like tail.

Big brown bat. A large bat, brown all over with naked ear and wing membranes, this species is most common around buildings and mine shafts. It is one of the earliest species to come out, usually before the sky gets dark.

Black bear. The most common of the American bears, the black bear is large and usually black or dark brown. It has a very small tail. Black bears lack the shoulder hump present on the larger grizzly bear. Black bears may not live in the Santa Ana Mountains and certainly are not native to the range. A string of sightings over the past fifty years makes one wonder. One legend holds that a circus bear escaped near the city of Corona and made its way into the mountains. More factual and telling, however, is the discovery of a pair of black bear cubs on the eastern slope above the town of Murrieta. No mother was ever found. I have, on two separate occasions, seen scat that I would bet a paycheck was from a bear.

Black rat. A brownish black of various shades with a long tail and a long, thin body, the black rat is found below 2,500 feet, especially around human dwellings. This rat is an introduced alien.

Black-tailed jackrabbit. This rabbit has long legs, long ears and fluffy white tail. Its body is light gray to brown and lighter underneath. This is the largest rabbit in the range and is much less common than the smaller rabbits listed elsewhere.

Bobcat. This species is the most common cat in the range. The bobcat—or lynx, as it is also known—is a grayish brown cat with dark spotting. Its tail is a stub, and its ears are tufted. Often, this tall, slender cat has been known to mix with domesticated felines. I have seen domestic cats and bobcats together around Blue Jay campground.

Brush mouse. This medium-sized brown mouse has a long tail and medium-sized ears. It is common in Manzanita and Ceonothus stands.

Brush rabbit. This small rabbit has short legs, pointed ears and a white rump and tail. Its body is brown, lighter underneath. Its tail is less full than that of the cottontail. It also prefers dense brush but probably lives higher in the range than the Audubon's cottontail.

Cactus mouse. This is a small mouse with soft, loose fur. It is brownish red with long tail and well adapted for arid desert environments.

California (brown) bat. A small reddish brown bat with medium-sized ears rising just above the top of the head, this species is common in Oak Woodlands. Its ears and face are dark brown or black.

California ground squirrel. This squirrel has a brown body with lighter speckling, white shoulders and a dark "V" on its back. It is common in the range, especially near disturbances.

California pocket mouse. This large mouse has long ears and a lighter belly, with stiff white hairs on its rump and sides. It is darker than the San Diego species described later on.

Coyote. The "song dog," the coyote is the hardiest of western predators. A medium-sized dog, its colors vary greatly but usually are brownish red with darker markings. It can be seen at any time but is mainly active at night. Coyotes do well around some human habitation. They are the only major predator in North America to expand their range and population numbers despite efforts to decrease their numbers or eliminate them entirely.

Wood rat nests like this one can be found throughout the woodlands and chaparral of the range.

Deer mouse. A small brown mouse, this species is distinguished by its short, bicolored tail. It also has medium-sized ears. It is found in all habitats at every elevation in the range. This mouse has gained significant notoriety over the past decade or so as the carrier of Hantavirus.

Desert shrew. This is a small gray or grayish brown shrew with a short tail. It has reddish teeth and large ears.

Dusky-footed wood rat. This species is a grayish brown, medium sized wood rat. Its tail is nearly bald and lightly bicolored. It is found in Chaparral, Oak Woodlands and other brush-covered habitats. Wood rats are also known as pack rats because they collect twigs, leaves and other debris to build their homes at the base of mature shrubs and trees. These homes can become quite large. I have seen them five to six feet high and at least that wide at the base. They often collect the things we drop to decorate their homes.

Gray fox. This little fox is gray with a light brown neck and legs and a long, narrow snout. It can climb trees well and is found in Woodlands and

Chaparral communities and in canyon bottoms. The gray fox is the only native fox in the Santa Ana Mountains. Traps and poison meant for coyotes often kill foxes instead. Gray fox are becoming rarer in the range.

Harvest mouse. This small brown mouse has a long tail and white belly. Its rounded ears are large, and it has a bicolored tail and the occasional buffy spot on its chest. It prefers grassy areas and avoids forests.

Hoary bat. A deep, dull brown with frosted tips on its dorsal hairs, this species is a fairly large migrating bat. Found in densely wooded areas, it feeds early in evening, often before dark.

House mouse. A small dark brown mouse with lighter underside, this species has a long, practically hairless tail. It is abundant worldwide but an alien here. The house mouse is especially successful around human habitation.

Long-tailed weasel. Brown with a black face and tip of the tail and lighter underneath, this species is mainly nocturnal but is sometimes active in the day. It is a ferocious predator.

Meadow vole. This is a medium-sized, grayish brown vole with a lightly bicolored tail. It prefers wet meadows below 4,500 feet. I have found this vole on the edge of wetlands and in overwatered "lawns."

Mountain lion. The mountain lion is the largest cat in the United States. Blond, red or golden brown, it can grow to between 85 to 160 pounds, with the occasional male reaching 200 pounds. It has a long slender tail and is six to eight feet from head to tail. Young cats have spotted fur until approximately six months of age. Mountain lions are easily distinguished by their long tail, even in young cats. The Santa Ana Mountains currently support anywhere from one to three dozen mountain lions. These animals are also called cougars, pumas and panthers.

There have been several lion attacks in the Santa Ana Mountains over the past several decades as mature cats seek food or water in an ever-shrinking range. In my years of exploring the slopes of Old Saddleback, I have seen only one mountain lion clearly; however, they have seen me much more often. Once, while studying recreational impacts in the San Mateo Canyon Wilderness, I spent a very uneasy day. It was as though I were not alone. The eerie feeling of being followed or stalked hung heavy on my shoulders as I followed trails and measured campsites. I would stop and wait for whoever it was behind me to appear, and they wouldn't. This process of looking over my shoulder, stopping and waiting—to no avail—continued all day.

Finally, as the sun set, I laid out my small tarp, sleeping pad and bag and then cooked a quick meal before climbing in my bag to go to sleep. As I awoke the following morning, I was shocked to find cougar prints across the sand coming right up to where my head was and then turning and heading off into the woods. I didn't have that eerie feeling again and haven't since.

Mule deer. This golden-brown deer is common in the range. Its tail is black tipped and its rump is white. Females are antlerless; males are larger and have antlers. Its large, pointed ears are mule-like.

Northern flying squirrel. Grayish brown with white-tipped hairs on its belly, a flap of skin between the hind and front legs allows this species to glide through the air. It is the only strictly nocturnal squirrel. I have personally never seen this species in the range, but I have seen several credible reports, so it is included.

Norway rat. Brown with rough fur, a naked tail and large bald ears, the Norway rat is common around buildings and agriculture. It is also an introduced species.

Opossum. The only marsupial in North America, the opossum has a gray body, naked tail and nearly naked face. It plays dead when harassed, though it may also hiss and snap if provoked. It is found at lower elevations and around human habitation in the Santa Ana Mountains.

Ornate shrew. This is a small, light-brown, long-tailed shrew with a vaguely bicolored tail.

Pacific kangaroo rat. A fairly large kangaroo rat with five toes on its rear feet. The base of its ears are white, and it has a dark tuft on its tail. Like most K-rats, it is distinctively dark above and light below. It prefers Chaparral communities with sandy soil and is common on the east slope around 1,800 to 2,500 feet.

Pallid bat. This species is a medium-sized bat with blond fur, sometimes with dark tips, and very long ears. It moves seasonally but doesn't migrate; it prefers open areas.

Parasitic mouse. The largest "deer mouse" in the state, this species is dark brown with a long tail. It is found in Oak Woodlands.

Pocket gopher. This enemy of every gardener has cheek pouches for carrying food and four "buck" teeth. It is a burrower and the only gopher in the range.

Raccoon. Salt-and-pepper gray, with a ringed tail and a conspicuous black eye mask, the raccoon is primarily nocturnal, though it can be seen often in early morning daylight as it returns from a night's work. Raccoons are usually solitary, except when breeding and raising young. They are known to wash their food before eating it.

Red bat. Bright reddish-brown with white-tipped dorsal hairs and large ears, the red bat is found in or near deciduous woodlands (canyon bottoms in our area). It starts to feed at high altitudes before dark, moving lower as the sun sets.

Red fox. Reddish brown and often fairly bright colored, the tip of the red fox's tail is white, and its feet are dark. It was introduced to Southern California and the Santa Ana Mountains. One report suggests that it was brought in by James Irvine for his hunting "pleasure." Apparently, he wasn't a very good shot, and the red fox escaped death. Other reports suggest the regional fur farms raised the fox for its hide, and many of the animals out-foxed the farmers by escaping to freedom in the hills.

Ring-tailed cat. This species is cat-like but related to raccoons. It is a grayish brown, long, slender animal with eight rings on its tail and white eye patches. It is rarely seen in the range but is known to raid campsite kitchens.

San Diego pocket mouse. A medium-sized mouse, this species is brown on its back and head with a white underside and black, stiff hairs on its rump. It has a bicolored tail.

Southern California mole. A light gray, medium-sized mole, this species has a naked nose, feet and tail. A burrower, it is active anytime but rarely seen above ground. It is the only mole in the range.

Southern grasshopper mouse. A reddish-brown mouse with a white belly and a thick, short tail, this species prefers a sandy habitat and is well adapted to desert environments.

Spotted skunk. Not really spotted, this skunk is rather extensively striped on its sides and back. It is more active than striped skunks and carries its tail in an erect position.

Striped skunk. Black with two white stripes down its back, the striped skunk has a large, bushy tail often raised in defense. It is common and can be found in all habitats in the Santa Ana Mountains. It is the chief carrier of rabies in our region.

Western gray squirrel. A large squirrel, gray all over with lighter-tipped hairs, especially on its tail, and a lighter belly, this bushy-tailed species is common in mature Oak Woodlands.

Western pipistrelle. Small and yellowish with black ears and face and short ears, this species is a mostly solitary bat found in open, arid areas.

I hope these basic descriptions help in your identification efforts but also give you a better understanding of the fauna of the Santa Ana Mountains. Happy tracking!

PART III

Hikes

Although this section has been named "Hikes," it really includes much more than that. This is the area of the book that you can use to put everything you learned in the rest of the book to use. The following pages include some of the best destinations in the range, although you are sure to discover many more on your own. You can also find contacts in this section to make additional connections with resource agencies, nonprofits and more. It also includes, of course, fourteen of the finest trails in the range.

DESTINATIONS

Southern Santa Ana Mountains

SANTA MARGARITA ECOLOGICAL RESERVE

The Santa Margarita River is one of Southern California's most important rivers. Its entire length deserves Wild and Scenic designation; however, because much of its winding path leads through Camp Pendleton Marine Corps Base, the public has no access to most of the river. The Santa Margarita River is home to many important species, including steelhead trout, which were seen spawning in the lower river as late as the 1990s; mountain lions; and a number of rare or threatened and endangered birds.

The Santa Margarita River is one of the last free-flowing rivers in Southern California. *Photo by Joel Robinson.*

The Santa Margarita Ecological Reserve represents the longest protected stretch of river in Southern California. The 4,344-acre river reserve was established in 1962 and is managed by San Diego State University. It covers more than five miles of the Santa Margarita River's length. As one of the university's field stations, the reserve serves as a research laboratory and outdoor classroom. These priorities also mean that the reserve is open only by reservation and on special event days such as watershed cleanups. Located just southwest of Temecula and north of Fallbrook, the Santa Margarita Reserve includes portions of San Diego and Riverside Counties.

The reserve is named for the river but has a diversity of habitats and includes deep canyon environments, among them the Temecula Gorge. Riparian forests of sycamore, willow and cottonwood make up the river bottom, while Southern Oak Woodland, Coastal Sage Scrub and Chaparral communities represent the upland habitats. A trip to the Santa Margarita Ecological Reserve will be one to remember, as it is really unlike any other area in the Santa Ana Mountains.

San Mateo Canyon Wilderness

San Mateo Canyon Wilderness is a forty-thousand-acre road-less wonderland. Its deep canyon bottoms are covered in old-growth oak woodlands and emerald green Riparian forests. Its slopes are carpeted in dense chaparral interrupted by occasion plateaus of grassland, and in spring, colorful wildflower displays emerge. A running creek and deep, cool, crisp pools dot the bottom of San Mateo Canyon most years; though in extreme drought, water may be limited to only a few locations.

Although the technical definition of a Wilderness area includes the phrase "absent of the works of man," San Mateo Canyon Wilderness has been inhabited by humans for centuries, and their works can be found pounded into granite boulders throughout the wilderness area. These deep depressions were created as acorns were ground into flour, and where the bedrock mortars are found, so usually are found ancient oak trees. San Mateo Canyon and its tributary canyons are no exception to this rule.

San Mateo Bottoms.

Wildlife abounds in the San Mateo Canyon Wilderness, which is home to mule deer, mountain lions, badgers and steelhead trout. In fact, an area at the confluence of Tenaja and San Mateo Creeks is know as Fisherman's Camp because until the 1970s you could drive to the bottom and car camp here. To this day, Fisherman's Camp is one of the most popular campsites in the wilderness, but now you can get there only on foot or hoof.

There are four main trailheads to access the San Mateo Canyon Wilderness. My favorite is the Tenaja Canyon trailhead. Historically, this area included a ranger station and campground; however, the area was closed in the 1990s due to poor conditions and minimal federal budgets.

Now, the trailhead includes paved parking, pit toilets and fresh well water. *Tenaja* is a Spanish word meaning "bowl," and the canyon is filled with stone bowls that hold water much of the year.

About three miles north is the Tenaja Falls trailhead. This location is popular because Tenaja Falls is the largest in the mountain range, and it can be reached in less than a mile from this parking area. In summer, this trailhead is busy and is often the site of illegal mountain bike and motorcycle access.

Tenaja Falls drops over more than one hundred feet of Batholithic granite and, when running, can be quite spectacular. Several great campsites can be found along the Tenaja Falls Trail north of the falls and south of Stewart Ranch, a large private in-holding surrounded by Wilderness.

Indian Potrero Trail is another of my favorites, although accessing it is often a complex process. The trailhead for Indian Potrero is located on the edge of Rancho Carillo, a private gated community several miles off Ortega Highway. Arrangements can be made with the U.S. Forest Service to access the area, but no vehicle parking is allowed in the community, so hikers have to be dropped off. Indian Potrero Trail is the westernmost trail in the Cleveland National Forest and at points offers views of the surf along the San Clemente and San Onofre coastline.

Bear Canyon Trail.

Farther up Ortega Highway, hikers and equestrians can access the San Mateo Canyon Wilderness from the San Juan Loop parking area, which is on the north side of Ortega Highway. The Bear Canyon trailhead is across the little two-lane highway next to the Ortega Candy Store. This quaint little historic outpost has the most basic supplies, like lemon heads, which I try to never hike without. Also available are books on the region and other information. Picnic tables are provided, and the store carries cold drinks to chill hot and tired hikers.

The Morgan trailhead is the fourth and final trailhead providing public access to the San Mateo Canyon Wilderness. It can be reached from the South Main Divide Road about two miles south of Ortega Highway. The trail is described in detail in the "Trails" section.

Ortega Corridor (San Juan Capistrano to Lake Elsinore)

Only one road safe enough for the average passenger car crosses the Santa Ana Mountains. That road is Ortega Highway, and if you have the time, it can be a spectacular trip. Don't drive this road if you are in a hurry. There is too much to see, and its conditions can be unpredictable. The highway has one lane in each direction and very few pullouts or stretches that allow for passing.

I lived at the top of Ortega Highway for nearly two years, and I spent many nights at the base of the road in San Juan Capistrano waiting for Caltrans to clear an accident so I could get home. On the weekends, this is a favorite trip for motorcyclists, some of whom ride way too fast, and inevitably

San Juan Canyon below Ortega Highway.

one of them crashes. I have missed appointments because we were stopped on the road, having already made it too far down to turn around but not far enough to take an alternative route.

Luckily, Ortega Highway is surrounded by spectacular views and is rich in natural and cultural history. Anywhere you stop on this road there is plenty to see. We will follow the road here, beginning in San Juan Capistrano and ending in the city of Lake Elsinore, and describe some of the sites and destinations worth a longer, slower look than is offered by highway speeds.

Ortega Highway really starts at the Mission San Juan Capistrano, which even today is at the heart of the community and a major tourist destination. From the road, one can see the remains of the old church, which had its beginnings way back in 1776. Inside the tall adobe walls, one can see many artifacts, gardens and other cultural elements relating to the start of what was to become Orange County. The mission often has classes and living history performances, so calling ahead is recommended to help you plan your trip over the mountain.

Leaving the quaint streets of San Juan Capistrano and heading east, travelers will immediately begin the ascent into the Santa Ana Mountains. Approximately one mile east of the mission, the Para Adobe and the Home of the San Juan Historic Society stands on your right. This unassuming white adobe building has only a small sign to describe its history, but it still stands out among the tract homes that surround it. The civilized world continues for another mile stretch to the intersection of Antonio Parkway. On your right is the Rancho Mission Viejo Equestrian Park and Event Center. Here, the hunter-jumper English-style equestrians compete for big money throughout the year.

Crossing Antonio Parkway, the highway begins to really climb as it bends and curves to the contour of the ever-steepening hills. This is the Rancho Mission Viejo, the last of the old ranches in Orange County. It is likely that you will see cattle mingling with mule deer as you continue your drive. In a few miles, Tree of Life Nursery and Caspers Wilderness Park will be on your left.

Only God grows more California native plants then Tree of Life Nursery, but it's not the quantity of plants that makes this place worth a visit; it's the people and their service. The retail area is exquisitely put together and promotes a lifestyle as much as a product. All of the buildings here are straw-bale constructed, and the staff members are always more than willing to discuss the process they went through to build them. The book selection is also worth a browse.

Next door to Tree of Life is Caspers Wilderness Park. This eight-thousand-acre park is a great place to camp, especially if you have horses. There are miles of trails to ride, bike and hike, and wildlife abounds here. There are many cultural sites in this area, and this was the original location for the Mission San Juan Capistrano. The Acjachemen tribe holds its annual picnic here in August.

The park is truly a wild experience, with deep canyons, old oaks and plenty of scenic vistas. A great nature center is open every day and includes some hands-on activities and a knowledgeable staff.

Reentering the highway from Caspers Park, one comes to Hot Springs Canyon after a mile or so. Just prior to Hot Springs Canyon Road is the actual hot springs, which once was a commercial operation but has been in disrepair and closed to the public for decades. Hot Springs Canyon is privately owned, but the owners allow access to the upper canyon for all those who are caring enough to ask. This canyon has nearly 80 percent of the plant species found in the range within in its steep walls, and at the head of the canyon is the largest waterfall in the range, at 140 feet. It's well worth a visit for the botanically minded, and golden eagles have been known to nest near the falls. The Los Pinos Trail parking and trailhead are here also.

Five or six miles up the highway from Hot Springs Canyon, you will come to Upper San Juan Campground, which is the first of several U.S. Forest Service campgrounds on Ortega Highway. Check with the forest service before planning a trip to this campground because its hours of operation are limited to peak days and seasons.

Another mile up, one finds the San Juan Loop parking area, Ortega Candy Store and Ortega Oaks RV Park. Numerous trails, including the San Juan Loop and Chiquito Basin and Bear Canyon Trails, can be accessed from here, and there are restrooms available at the parking area. The candy store really is a candy store, with fresh homemade fudge, jawbreakers and more. You can get other souvenirs, books, a cold soda and even a fresh sandwich here. If you like, there is almost always space for rent at the RV park.

Just above the candy store and after a steep and sharp S-turn on the highway is a pullout and parking area for Ortega Falls. This area has been poorly treated in the past and is known locally as a party spot, though the U.S. Forest Service and many volunteers have cleaned it up in recent years. The falls are small but easily accessed. This is also a popular climbing location.

Another short drive up the highway is Acjachemen Meadow on the right side of the road. This meadow is a historic gathering area for local native basket makers, and it provides access to Decker Canyon as well. This is sacred ground, so treat it with the utmost respect.

The closest thing to a mountain town in the Santa Ana Mountains is El Cariso Village. Like most mountain towns, this village has its share of artists and vagabonds, but it is also a haven for bikers. The only bar or restaurant in town is Hell's Kitchen, though there is also a deli across the street. Both have outside dining and serve cold beer. The town is complete with a fire station, two forest service campgrounds, a visitors' center and a nature trail.

Just east of El Cariso Village is the Main Divide Road. Turn left here and you go to Blue Jay Campground and Falcon Group Camp or continue all the way to Santiago Peak. Turn right and you pass the Rancho Capistrano horse community on your way to Wildomar OHV Camp and trailheads for the San Mateo Canyon Wilderness.

If you pass Main Divide Road, you begin the descent into Lake Elsinore. But before you drop in elevation too much, there is a pullout on the left that overlooks the lake from two thousand feet above. This turnout is not the safest place to cross the highway for eastbound traffic, but do not fear. Just down the highway a quarter mile is the Lookout, a roadhouse with a large parking lot and equally impressive views. This place is also popular with the motorcycle crowd but has good food and outside dining.

Finally, the highway begins a curvy and steep drop into Lake Elsinore, where boating, fishing and other water sports can be experienced on the largest sag pond in California. Although Highway 74 continues across the Elsinore and Hemet Valleys, Ortega Highway ends here.

CASPERS WILDERNESS PARK

Orange County has a habit of naming parks after former supervisors, and Caspers Wilderness Park is no different. In this case, it is named for Supervisor Ronald Caspers, who mysteriously disappeared while on a fishing trip to Baja, Mexico, in 1974. The sixty-foot ship he was on registered a mayday call on the night of June 13, and that was the last anyone heard from the ten passengers onboard. Half the passengers were county political powerhouses, and many people believe that the accident and subsequent disappearance have never adequately been solved.

My father was a lieutenant with the Orange County Sheriff's Department and a volunteer for the Civil Air Patrol, and I remember him going away for some time searching for Mr. Caspers. The park has always stood out to me for that reason. After visiting the park, it will stand out for you, too, as this is one spectacular piece of property.

Most of this park was once part of the Starr Ranch, a hobby cattle operation covering nearly ten thousand acres. Eugene Starr, who made his money in oil, divided his ranch between the County of Orange and the National Audubon Society, creating two of the most important preserves in the Santa Ana Mountains.

As mentioned earlier, this park covers more than four thousand acres and is one of the best examples of the wild Santa Ana Mountains outside the San Mateo Canyon Wilderness. With its boundaries reaching north to Starr Ranch Audubon Sanctuary, east to Hot Springs Canyon and south well across Ortega Highway to the borders of the San Mateo Canyon Wilderness Area, an exploration of this park is worthy of a multi-day trip.

Luckily, Caspers is also home to one of the finest campgrounds in the range and can accommodate large rigs and trailers, making the overnighter a pleasant experience all the way around. There are even showers at the campground. The campground at Caspers Wilderness Park is also the best public horse camping opportunity in the Santa Ana Mountains, with pull-through trailer spots and corrals at each location. The horse camp is also separate from the rest of the campground, keeping horses and campers safe.

Mature oak woodlands, seasonal creeks, coastal sage scrub and grasslands cover most of this park. Unique geological features here make for interesting views, and this is a popular spot for plein air painters and nature photographers, as well as the casual observer who just wants to get away.

Native American history in this park and surrounding areas is evident by the cultural sites encountered as one explores the area. Bell Canyon was likely one of the most heavily used areas by native people prior to the Spanish rule of the area. Even today, the Acjachemen tribe holds an annual reunion here.

Whether you visit Caspers for a day or week, and whether on foot, bike or horse, there are miles of trails to cover, dozens of vistas to view and even a great little visitors' center. Call for access and prices as this is a county facility and hours and costs may vary.

East Side

OLD TOWN TEMECULA

Resting at the southeastern foot of the Santa Ana Mountains is Old Town Temecula. It seems like today, every town has an old town, but not many are as old as Old Town Temecula. This five-block area has been updated since its inception, but it still feels like you have stepped back into the Old West when you step onto the street here. Once a village of the Pechanga band of Payomkowishum or Luiseno Indians, the town came of age with the ranchos and cattle booms of the early and mid-1800s.

Today, the buildings house high-end boutiques, novelty shops and restaurants instead of saloons and general mercantile stores; however, Old Town Temecula still has a feed store, clothing stores and a fair share of watering holes. Several hotels are nearby as well. There is even a museum and theater here that hosts regular productions of the classics from Broadway, as well as original productions from local playwrights.

Old Town Temecula is a great place to end a long hike or horseback ride in the Santa Ana Mountains. Or make it your base for the Temecula Valley balloon and wine festival. Several times each year, the town closes the streets of Old Town to host fairs and festivals, so check with the local chamber of commerce when planning your trip.

SANTA ROSA PLATEAU

The Santa Rosa Plateau is Old California at its best. Just getting to the entrance of the park is like driving back in time. Of course, you have to ignore the mega mansions that have sprung up along the road in the last couple of decades, but that is one of the charms of the Santa Rosa. Once you are in the park, the scenery is so breathtaking that the outside world no longer exists. At nearly nine thousand acres, the park is an easy place to get away from the hustle and bustle of the new California.

The Santa Rosa Plateau boasts numerous highlights, including the most vernal pools in the Santa Ana Mountains, the largest stand of Engelmann oaks on earth and extensive native grasslands. The preserved land is home to forty-nine Threatened and Endangered plant and animal species. The geology of the Santa Rosa Plateau is also of interest and is visible from the Elsinore-Temecula Valleys below.

Santa Rosa Plateau vernal pool. *Photo by Joel Robinson.*

Once a sprawling cattle ranch, today the area is cattle-free but still equestrian friendly. The Santa Rosa Plateau Foundation, which raises funds for the educational programs at the park, is the sponsor and beneficiary of an annual National Day of the Cowboy event that highlights the area's cowboy and vaquero heritage. The park is home to the Moreno and Machado Adobes, which add to the Old California flavor of the area.

In addition to horseback riding, mountain biking and hiking are also popular activities on the plateau. The Santa Rosa Plateau is one of my favorite bird-watching locations, with more than two hundred species having been identified on the site. The park's many raptors are a highlight of any visit.

The Santa Rosa Plateau has had many property owners or managers over time, beginning with the Luiseno Indians who lived in and utilized the area into the late 1800s. The region, including the nearby Cleveland National Forest, still has evidence of these first residents of the range in the form of bedrock mortars and rock art. The area was also important as a source of basket-weaving materials.

By the middle of the nineteenth century, the Santa Rosa was a rancho in all of the splendor of the post-mission era. It remained a cattle operation well into the twentieth century, when the cities of Murrieta and Temecula began developing. In the 1980s, the Nature Conservancy began buying up the Santa Rosa Plateau and planning for a wildlife corridor that would connect the Santa Ana Mountains with core habitat areas to the southeast. The area also proved important as a movement corridor for mountain lions, deer and other large mammals within the Santa Ana Mountains. Eventually, California Fish and Game received ownership and deeded the property to the capable people of the Riverside County Open Space and Parks District who own and manage the reserve today.

LAKE ELSINORE

The city of Lake Elsinore's motto is "Dream Extreme," and it does. Here you can water ski or wake board behind a speeding boat or float slowly along a cove, fishing for large-mouth bass. You can jump out of an airplane at ten thousand feet in the air or fly over jumps on a motorcycle.

Lake Elsinore.

You can even jump off the side of the of the Santa Ana Mountains with wings of your own.

Lake Elsinore is a natural lake or sag pond, which means water rises to the surface through fissures in the ground caused by activity along the Elsinore-Whittier Fault. The San Jacinto River also terminates here, but due to drought and groundwater pumping, neither source puts a lot of water in the lake. For many years, Lake Elsinore was nothing more than a large mud puddle. At other times, there was too much water, and the town surrounding the lake would flood. Today, the Elsinore Valley Municipal Water District uses imported water from the Colorado River and a series of dikes and channels to control the water levels in Lake Elsinore. The results of this effort are improved water quality, new recreation opportunities and a better aquatic habitat.

Although the city and chamber of commerce promote Lake Elsinore as a resort town, efforts toward this end are limited. There are a few motels next to the casino on the southeast end of the lake and a couple campgrounds on the north shore, but little else is in place to bring this area into the primetime. This is not to say that Lake Elsinore isn't worth a visit, because it is.

The nature lover will find plenty here to meet his needs. There is no better place in the Greater Santa Ana Mountains to see shorebirds, and the miles of shoreline offer up herons, egrets and sandpipers. The extensive Riparian Woodlands and marshes to the north and south of the lake promise a tropical surprise, including yellow warblers, yellow-breasted chats and even, on rare occasions, a vermillion flycatcher.

Lake Elsinore is a great place to stage extensive trips into the backcountry as well. Ortega Highway and Interstate 15 provide many access points into the mountains and San Mateo Canyon Wilderness. I often end my wilderness trips with pizza and beer in one of Lake Elsinore's many restaurants.

GLEN IVY HOT SPRINGS/TEMESCAL HISTORICAL MARKERS

For more than 150 years, Glen Ivy Hot Springs has been welcoming the weary traveler. Today, you can stay only for the day, but in its heyday, Glen Ivy served overnight guests, many of whom were taking a break from the long trip on the Butterfield Stage Route. Perhaps that service will return one day. For now, though, Glen Ivy is a luxurious yet friendly resort-style day spa, with almost a dozen pools, including the famed mineral pools that bubble up from deep beneath the Santa Ana Mountains and emerge here at more than one hundred degrees Fahrenheit.

You can get a massage or have your nails done here. You can even get a great meal from Café Sole, the inside eatery at Glen Ivy. Whatever you do at Glen Ivy, remember that this place would not exist were it not for the Santa Ana Mountains that surround it. The hot water comes from deep beneath them, the cold water rolls down Coldwater Canyon from high above, and without that combination of waters, Glen Ivy would not exist. As you lie there floating in one of Glen Ivy's pools, I encourage you to enjoy the lush and creative landscape. (I, along with a team of others, took care of it for nearly three years.) Then look up and enjoy the breathtaking view that is the Santa Ana Mountains.

Also, remember that for more than nine thousand years, people have been using and enjoying the sacred and healing waters at the mouth of Coldwater Canyon. Legend suggests that no particular tribe claimed Coldwater Canyon and its hot waters, but instead, it was shared by all who needed it. No local people inhabited Coldwater Canyon even though it contained great water and wonderful oak woodlands. Coldwater Canyon was known as a favorite haunt of mama grizzly bears and their cubs. Native people instead preferred the lower rolling hills around what is now Tom's Farms.

Serrano Plaque.

It wasn't until the early 1800s, when Leandro Serrano built the first non-indigenous home in Riverside County, that the area was settled and the canyon inhabited on a nearly permanent basis. Serrano's widow stayed on the land until 1898. His descendants also settled ranchos on the west side of old Saddleback. Today, two tanning vats originally built by local natives at Leandro Serrano's direction have been restored by local Boy Scouts. The vats and historic signs can be found just east of Interstate 15 on the south side of Temescal Road.

TIN MINE CANYON

Tin Mine Canyon got its name from the tin mines that operated in the area, although little or no tin was actually extracted from this side of the Santa Ana Mountains (or maybe from either side of the range, for that matter). That being said, this narrow and steep canyon is still worthy of exploration. The dense brush makes for slow going in the upper reaches, while a semi-developed trail exists in the lower reach.

Trails4All, a nonprofit trail-building, maintenance and educational organization, has been working with the forest service to improve this area. A trip up Skyline Drive, which begins at the mouth of Tin Mine Canyon and follows the north ridge of the canyon up to the Main Divide Road, provides excellent views into Tin Mine Canyon. Either route—the road or the canyon bottom—is worthy of a full-day trip, so plan accordingly. Bring water!

Tin Mine Canyon.

135

West Side

Riley Wilderness Park

This little wilderness park is home to some of the finest oak trees I've ever seen. In addition, there are two seasonal creeks with well-developed Riparian areas. Coastal Sage Scrub habitat covers the uplands. Named after a former county supervisor who, ironically, was no friend to the county's wilderness, Riley Wilderness Park is hidden at the top of Oso Parkway near Coto de Caza.

Whiting Ranch/Limestone Canyon Wilderness Park

Whiting Ranch and Limestone Canyon Wilderness Park is a mountain biker's heaven. Steep trails and fewer hikers than other parks in the area make this one of the region's best biking opportunities.

Once a sprawling cattle ranch, Whiting Ranch still retains some of the remnants of the old ranch. Dwight Whiting acquired ten thousand acres of Rancho Canada de los Alisos from the Serranos, who had fallen on hard financial times. The Whiting family lived there well into the mid-1900s and ran cattle there until donating the land to the county.

What makes this park interesting, however, is not the ranching history; it's the geology. Steep and colorful sedimentary layers have become exposed, creating canyons, grottos and mini badlands reminiscent of Arizona and Utah, not Southern California. In fact, Limestone Canyon is home to the "Sinks," a two-hundred-foot-deep canyon known as Orange County's Grand Canyon.

Today, the park covers 4,300 acres and connects with the Irvine Ranch Conservancy's open space lands. Whiting Ranch would be a great starting point for a multiday excursion through the lower Santa Ana Mountains and canyons.

Trabuco and Holy Jim Canyons

Trabuco and Holy Jim Canyons are an unexpected surprise in Southern California. One would expect to experience these places in the Santa Cruz Mountains or the Coast Ranges north of San Francisco but not down here in dry Southern California. Giant chain fern, madrone and big-cone Douglas fir forests cover the slopes of these canyons. Although on occasion the streams dry up, this watershed feels moist, like its cousins to the north.

Trabuco Canyon was named by the Portola Party who lost a Trabuco rifle there in 1769. The name has been tagged on this drainage ever since. Holy Jim Canyon, on the other hand, has a less innocent namesake: James T. Smith, who was widely known as Cousin Jim for his unmistakable vocabulary. Mapmakers were uneasy with the name Cousin Jim, so they conveniently changed the name of this canyon to Holy Jim Canyon.

Trabuco Canyon is the only canyon in the Santa Ana Mountains dominated by Conifer Forest communities, at least in view, if not number. Big-cone Douglas fir and Coulter pine grow throughout the canyon, with Coulter pine becoming more abundant in the upper canyon. Cedar and Monterey pine can be found in the higher reaches of the canyon and were introduced by tree-planting programs. A little more than halfway up the canyon, Yeager Mesa is visible on the opposite slope of the trail. Now covered primarily with ferns, the mesa was once used as pasture by the U.S. Forest Service. Jake Yeager, an early miner in the canyon, had a cabin nearby. Remnants of his gold and silver claims can still be seen along the trail and throughout the canyon. Yeager Mesa was purchased by a land trust a few years ago and will likely be given to the forest service.

Holy Jim Canyon is as unique, if not as large, as Trabuco Canyon. Instead of conifer woodlands, however, the forests of this canyon are dominated by oaks. Some of the largest ferns I've ever seen grow around Bear Springs, about midway up this canyon, and this is the easiest and shortest route to Santiago Peak.

O'NEILL REGIONAL PARK

This little park has wonderful Riparian areas and a great campground. Covering portions of Trabuco and Live Oak Canyons, there are numerous quality picnic areas and a visitors' center. The stone work in the park dates back to the 1930s and has the Conservation Corps look associated with many of the older parks in the mountains.

Development in the past couple decades has severely encroached on this park, making O'Neill Regional Park feel less natural and wild. Don't, however, let that get in the way of making this park a day trip or overnight destination. Some of my best car camping experiences are from O'Neill. It also serves well as a staging area for multiday explorations of the western canyons. Set up camp and then take short commutes up Trabuco or Modjeska Canyons, returning for a great meal and some rest under the stars.

Wildlife is abundant in O'Neill Regional Park. I have encountered coyotes, raccoons and rabbits on every overnight visit for the past twenty years. If you camp, keep your food put away, as the critters will come at night.

MODJESKA CANYON (ARDEN AND TUCKER WILDLIFE SANCTUARY)

Modjeska Canyon is one of the most quaint and picturesque communities in the Santa Ana Mountains. Its narrow road, which in places is barely wide enough to provide for a lane in each direction of travel, winds around properties with signs that read "Watch for Children" and "Chicken Crossing." Though many of the properties are not on large lots, there is no question that this is rural living. Some homes are quite large, while others appear to be mere cabins. Old cars rest on the lawn of one, while a custom-manicured landscape covers the next. Goats and horses can be seen grazing in front of a few of the homes, while dogs often curl up in the road in front of others, oblivious to traffic and other dangers.

The canyon is named for Helena Modjeska, a famed Polish actress who came to the canyon around 1887 to build her home, which she called the Forest of Arden. Today, Arden is a county historic site and park open to visitors. During Modjeska's time, the property was a struggling olive operation. The limbs of the Madame's grove still stretch across the road that leads into the canyon today. Pay close attention to signs if you are looking for the Modjeska House, as it is easy to miss from the road. Once you have found it, however, you will not soon forget it.

Don't plan a visit to Modjeska Canyon without making Tucker Wildlife Sanctuary one of your stops. This great little nature retreat is located near the end of the canyon's road and is owned and operated by California State University–Fullerton. The facility is staffed mostly by students whose passion and interest in the Santa Ana Mountains is worth making the connection, even if you spend little time in the sanctuary itself.

On the north side of the road is a small interpretive center and a signed nature trail known as the Braille Trail because its signs are embossed in Braille for the sight-impaired. This is also the access point for Harding Truck Trail and Canyon. On the south side is the main body of the sanctuary, complete with a "viewing patio" that has been baited with bird feeders and can be a great place to watch birds and other wildlife. Two ponds and an amphitheater are also present here. Santiago Creek runs through the property; here, it is also known as Modjeska Creek.

Whether you stop at Arden or Tucker, as the locals refer to them, a visit to the west side is not complete without a drive into Modjeska Canyon.

SILVERADO CANYON

This is one crazy place. You never know whom or what you might run into here. It is this unpredictability, though, that makes Silverado Canyon such a great place. From the 1870s boom years to the present, Silverado Canyon has been a community of characters—some with big ideas they hoped to share with the world. Other characters who came to Silverado did so to get away from everything and everyone. Some wanted to develop the canyon, while others vowed to fight even the smallest project. That is the definition of community, and in Silverado Canyon, it plays out every Tuesday night at the Silverado Café, which also makes a great breakfast. I recommend the huevos rancheros.

If you like horses, Carbondale Stables is worth a quick look, although it really was more fun when the stables still hosted the Silverado Cattle Club on Friday nights. If you stop in, say hello to Rob the ranch hand and tell him Patrick sent you. The stables actually sit on the site of the town of Carbondale. The old barn may even date back to the days of Carbondale's boom.

The Silverado Community Center hosts great lectures and special events. It is also the home of canyon-wide meetings when the community wants to discuss big issues. Another important community facility is the library, which is next to the liquor store. The library isn't big, but it does have a great collection of historical photos and artifacts.

Continue up the canyon to the Maple Springs Visitors' Center, where volunteers staff the building and answer questions about the range and the canyon. Some of the naturalists who staff this little cabin-like facility are truly experts on the Santa Ana Mountains. Perhaps the most important of these local naturalists is my good friend Joel Robinson, who is unmistakably barefoot and often dressed more like Samuel Shrewsbury than the typical twenty-first-century naturalist. His organization, Naturalist For You, leads more free guided hikes and programs in the Santa Ana Mountains than the U.S. Forest Service has firefighters. He makes his home in Ladd Canyon, just off Silverado Canyon Road, and makes Silverado Canyon the base of his operations.

No matter when you go or where you stop in Silverado, you are sure to have an experience to remember.

BLACK STAR CANYON AND THE MARIPOSA PRESERVE

Black Star Canyon is probably the least known of the major canyons on the western slope of the Santa Ana Mountains. This is mainly because it lies behind a locked gate. This gate is only to keep automobiles out, not to prevent hikers, bicyclists or equestrians from exploring the canyon. There have been a few locals who would have visitors believe otherwise. I have even been stopped at gunpoint and chased by large dogs. This was all in the past, however, as new major landowners and a more informed community have discovered Black Star Canyon.

In the 1970s and '80s, Black Star Canyon developed a notorious reputation for having a dark and mysterious ambiance. Rumors of satanic rituals and even a breathing rock spread to the base of the mountains and beyond. City kids dared one another to visit the canyon on Friday nights. Many did, myself among them. I was even told once that the name "Blackstar" came from the dark church that once existed at the mouth of the canyon. The name actually originated with the Black Star Coal Mine that incorporated in October 1876. The mine produced nearly ten tons of coal a day in its heyday.

Historic Hidden Ranch is now known as the Mariposa Preserve.

Mariposa lily.

About four miles up the canyon from the historic mine site rested the nine-hundred-acre Hidden Ranch. This quaint and quiet ranch sat on a grassy flat, lined by the sycamore-wooded Black Star Creek. Oak woodlands and chaparral covered the slopes.

Prior to both the mine and the ranch, however, the canyon was home to Tongva clans that collected acorns and seeds and hunted the small game that frequented the canyon. This came to an end when white settlers blamed the natives for stealing horses, and a massacre occurred.

Today, 897 acres have been purchased and preserved by the Wildlands Conservancy. They renamed the area the Mariposa Preserve because of the Mariposa lilies that are common on the old ranch property in spring and summer. The property is open for day use and must be reached by foot, bike or horse. Explore the old ranch and look for the Native American evidence that represents thousands of years of habitation.

IRVINE LAKE

Irvine Lake is a seven-hundred-acre reservoir that forms the largest body of water within the Santa Ana Mountains. Lake Elsinore is larger and

141

Under Irvine Lake.

geologically related to the range but rests at the foot of, rather than within, the Santa Ana Mountains. The reservoir we call Irvine Lake was originally created to provide water for the Irvine Ranch and its agricultural operations; however, as the ranch converted from farming and ranching to residential and commercial development, the lake now provides water for growing cities. It serves a flood control role as well, though that is not its primary purpose. Irvine Lake isn't just a water storage facility, though. The lake is open for fishing, and because it is privately owned, no license is required. There is a fee to enter and use the lake. Boats are allowed and can be rented at the lake.

If you don't fish, Irvine Lake also provides incredible views and is excellent for bird watching. There is a tiny café at the lake—a great place to relax and listen to the locals tell fish stories.

Speaking of fish stories, Irvine Lake is home to a rare fish, the three-spine stickleback. This prehistoric-looking species is native to the region but is found only in a few locations in Southern California. Other unique species can be found around the lake.

The lake often hosts special events such as concerts, car shows and tournaments of different types, so check the calendar or call in advance to see what's going on. I once went to watch the American white pelicans that frequent the lake and arrived to find a Harley Davidson rally going on. There wasn't a bird on the lake that day, but I got to see the original bikes from the movie *Easy Rider*, so it wasn't a total loss.

The lake hasn't always been there. In fact, where the Santiago Reservoir, as it is sometimes referred to in official circles, now rests was once a small structure used as a temporary home by Teodosio Yorba, owner of the Rancho Lomas de Santiago. Though the crude structure was only a small, wooden-framed square cover with brush, it was well situated and visited regularly. Once the Irvines acquired the Rancho Lomas, the site, which was then a wide, grassy valley shaded by sycamores, became a sheep and cow camp for the cowboys working the Irvine Ranch.

As you ply the waters or explore the shore of Irvine Lake, take in the views and imagine the times past, when Santiago Creek ran through the tranquil valley, lined by wide-spreading sycamores, grazed by pronghorn and hunted by wolf and bear.

IRVINE RANCH CONSERVANCY

The Irvine Ranch Conservancy protects more than fifty thousand acres of the historic Irvine Ranch, more than half of which is in or at the base of the Santa Ana Mountains. The conservancy operates with the mission of managing the lands with a balance of preservation and participation. In

Irvine Ranch
Conservancy.

other words, this means it limits access in the name of ecological protection. Guided hikes, bike rides and horseback rides are offered on most days. Open exploration days are offered a couple times a year on which visitors can enter the conservancy lands and explore at their own leisure.

The Irvine Ranch Conservancy is one of fewer than six hundred National Natural Landmarks. This designation has no regulatory protections but does call out the quality and uniqueness of the lands of the Irvine Ranch. The Irvine Ranch Conservancy gained the designation for its biological and geological characteristics.

My favorite part of the conservancy lands is Fremont Canyon. This natural landscape is as wild as any place I have ever explored. The narrows of this canyon have prevented cattle and other livestock from grazing the upper reaches, making these places as natural and wild as they were in 1769, when Portola wandered past the mouth of Fremont Canyon.

IRVINE REGIONAL PARK

In 1876, James Irvine Sr., the founder of the Irvine Ranch, donated 160 acres to the County of Orange to create Irvine Park, California's first regional park. At that time, the area was simply known as the "Picnic Grounds" and was a popular daytrip destination for the county's metropolitan set. Today, Irvine Regional Park has grown to nearly 500 acres and is one of the most popular parks in Orange County.

California's first regional park.

The line to enter often stretches almost a mile on holidays when the park fills up before noon and visitors have to be turned away. It is no surprise, though, once you enter the beautiful park, with its centuries-old coast live oak stands, huge sycamore trees that shade picnicking visitors and great views of the peaks and canyons of the northern Santa Ana Mountains. For the less casual park-goers, there are ball fields, hiking trails, a nature center and a zoo. The park has a small lake where shoreline fishing is permitted and pedal boats can be rented. A small narrow-gauge railroad runs through a portion of the park and takes visitors on a historic journey through the history of Irvine Park.

Joseph Pleasants, who was known more by his initials "J.E." than by his full name, was one of the earliest "gringos" to settle in the Santa Ana Mountains and made one of his homes in an oak grove in what is now Irvine Park. He later went on to live in and around other canyons in the range but spent nearly seventy-five years living in the Santa Ana Mountains.

Those same oak groves discussed above were popular with bears, and in several accounts from the 1800s, black bears were identified there, not just grizzlies. This becomes interesting when one realizes that black bears have never naturally occurred south of the Tehachapi Mountains, except by introduction in the early 1900s to the San Gabriel and San Bernardino Mountains. The ghosts of the Irvine Park black bears still leave their sign around the Santa Ana Mountains today. I have seen it myself, although it was much farther south in the range.

SANTIAGO OAKS REGIONAL PARK

Hidden in a quaint neighborhood above Santiago Creek lies the unheralded entrance to Santiago Oaks Regional Park. This park is actually made up of several parcels, all within the Santiago Creek Watershed. Beautiful oak groves, as well as Riparian Forests and Coastal Sage Scrub habitats, can be found in the park. Hiking, mountain biking and equestrian trails wind throughout the park. In fact, many of the homes that border the park are equestrian properties that utilize the park for trail rides.

There is a historic dam within the park that once provided water for local agricultural endeavors. There is a historic orange grove in the park that provides a lasting example of those efforts. The trees in that grove continue to provide commercial-sized harvests today.

The larger Villa Park Dam borders the park and is an important point of flood control along Santiago Creek. Behind this dam is an impressive Riparian woodland that is home to an incredible array of water birds and

The forks at Santiago Regional Park.

some endangered species that nest in the trees and shrubs. The area makes for some great bird watching.

Santiago Oaks is also home to a watershed education center. Because of the field trips provided at the center, children make up the park's largest visitor group.

North Side

STAR RANCH EVENT AND EQUESTRIAN CENTER

This facility is hidden on the northernmost slope of the range overlooking Santa Ana Canyon high above the Santa Ana River. From below, only the white three-rail ranch fence that follows the winding entrance road is visible. Upon entering. however, a historic ranch appears nestled among oaks and eucalyptus. Complete with the original homestead house and a re-created Mexican village, the facility is a great place to host celebrations of all kinds.

The owners also offer guided horseback riding trips from the ranch. Many of the trips come complete with dinner. You can also board your own horse there and ride into the mountains as far and as often as you wish.

Star Ranch.

Weddings are the primary business of this old ranch now, and the facility has several areas for special events. The view from any of the event areas is spectacular and sure to provide a memorable day.

CHINO HILLS STATE PARK, COAL CANYON SECTION

Chino Hills State Park protects nearly thirteen thousand acres and includes a portion of the Santa Ana Mountains in Coal Canyon. The Chino Hills and Santa Ana Mountains are connected in origin and are only separated by the Santa Ana River. Both the hills and the mountains were uplifted by geologic activity along the Elsinore-Whittier Fault.

Coal Canyon is important ecologically but also has great social significance. Most of the canyon was once slated for residential development. Then a biologist who studied mountain lions realized that Coal Canyon was the preferred crossing point of lions traveling between Chino Hills and the Santa Ana Mountains. If this crossing were lost, the Santa Ana Mountains' lion population would disappear, further upsetting the already strained and sensitive ecological balance. Activists, urban planners and developers squared off. Eventually, the Wildlands Conservancy purchased and protected the canyon. It was added to Chino Hills State Park, stretching it across the Santa Ana River and well into the Santa Ana Mountains.

What makes Coal Canyon so significant was an event that followed. Southern California is known for its addiction to the automobile and is famous for its freeways. Jammed between the Santa Ana Mountains and the Santa Ana River is the I-91 freeway. This route is well known for being a slow drive and often resembles a parking lot more than a road. Early in the twenty-first-century, the Coal Canyon on and off ramps were closed. For the first time in California's history, the Department of Transportation closed an off ramp and on ramp to protect wildlife.

If the state was willing to do that, the least we can do is visit Coal Canyon. This deep, north-facing canyon is home to the northernmost stand of Tecate cypress trees in the world, and maybe you will be lucky enough to see an elusive mountain lion.

Coal Canyon can be reached by parking at the end of Green River Road near the Green River Golf Course and following the Santa Ana River Trail to the mouth of Coal Canyon. From there you can follow Coal Canyon Truck Trail into and up the canyon.

SANTA ANA RIVER

The Santa Ana River is Southern California's largest river system, winding more than one hundred miles from the top of the San Bernardino Mountains to Huntington Beach and the Pacific Ocean. The Santa Ana River gets its name because the Portola Expedition of 1769 believed that the river originated in the Santa Ana Mountains, which they had named on Saint Anne's Day a few days prior to camping on the banks of the river.

At the northern foot of the Santa Ana Mountains, the Santa Ana River has carved a canyon between the range and the Chino hills to the north. Geologists call this area the Santa Ana Gap. In fact, the river predates the mountains and the hills and sliced away at the rock and soil as the land around it was uplifted along the Elsinore-Whittier Fault.

Santa Ana
Canyon.

The Santa Ana River Trail can be accessed here at Green River Road and downstream at Gypsum Canyon Road, as well as at the Canyon RV Park, previously know as Featherly Regional Park. Chino Hills State Park crosses the river at Coal Canyon and extends into the Santa Ana Mountains.

Where the Santa Ana River forms the boundary between the mountains and hills, it winds and bends as it flows under mature cottonwood and willow trees. Mule fat shrubs line the upper banks of the river, and sandy beaches form openings under the trees. Wildflowers bloom here in the spring and summer. Because of the controlled releases of water from behind Prado Dam, the river here is constant and always has visible flow.

The Santa Ana River Trail can be accessed here and walked or ridden downstream to the ocean or upstream through the Prado Basin and the Inland Empire of Riverside and San Bernardino Counties. Both paved and soft-surface trail are available along this stretch of the river.

Maybe, though, walking and riding aren't your idea of a good time? Well, you're in luck because several groups are currently working to establish rafting operations along the river. These trips will offer a one-of-a-kind experience for Southern California and its one-of-a-kind river.

Golfing is available along the river at the Green River Golf Course off Green River Road. Though I don't golf, I have always admired the scenery at this course. The mature cottonwoods here have been maintained so as to stand alone and demonstrate their furrowed majesty. For more information on the river and its access or recreational opportunities, contact the Orange County Harbors, Beaches and Parks Department or the Orange County Water District.

TRAILS

Tenaja Trail

The Tenaja Trail is one of my favorite trails in the San Mateo Canyon Wilderness. Beginning at the south end of the Wilderness area at the Tenaja trailhead and parking area, the trail quickly drops into Tenaja Canyon and crosses the creek a couple times before sticking to the west side of the canyon for most of the three-mile trip to Fisherman's Camp. This historic camp was once an auto camp but has renaturalized into a perfect trail camp. In winter, this descent can be quite wet, with the initial creek crossings likely to require wet boots. Poison oak is common along this trail, and so are wild peonies in late spring. March and April evenings along this trail are difficult as the trail and slope are covered in California newts.

From Fisherman's Camp, the trail crosses San Mateo Canyon and climbs quickly out of the canyon and into the chaparral. This route runs four miles to Four Corners, crossing great stands of chamise, broken by the occasional grassy flat and oak woodland. Wildflowers are common throughout this route for much of the spring and summer seasons. In late summer and fall, the direct sunlight on the trail can be quite hot. I recommend traversing this section early in the morning. From Four Corners, it is just a hop, skip and a jump to Pigeon Springs, where water is usually available. From there, Bear Canyon Trail takes you to Ortega Highway and the San Juan Loop parking area.

From Fisherman's Camp, hikers and equestrians have a choice of where to go. In addition to the northern section of Tenaja Trail, the San Mateo Trail can be accessed and will take you upstream to Tenaja Falls, one of the highest in the range, or downstream into the depths of San Mateo Canyon and the boundary of Camp Pendalton Marine Base.

As mentioned earlier, *Tenaja* is a Spanish word meaning "bowl" and refers to the rock bowls that have formed along the Tenaja Creek. These little pools hold water well into summer when there has been significant rain the preceding winter. Evidence of Native American habitation can be seen in Tenaja and San Mateo Canyons.

Morgan Trail

The Morgan Trail begins at the ridge of the range along the Southern Main Divide Road about two and a half miles south of Ortega Highway. This trail once had issues with off-road vehicles but today is in good shape for hikers. Except following rain, this trail has no available water, so bring your own.

The trail winds its way into Morrell Canyon and follows the creek for a distance of just less than one mile. At this point, hikers enter a beautiful oak woodland that has served as a trail camp for those getting a late start into the San Mateo Canyon Wilderness. From here, the trail leads out of Morrell Canyon and into the chaparral and grasslands of the Potrero country. In about another mile, hikers reach the Tenaja Falls Trail, which heads south, wrapping around the east side of the Stewart Ranch Property for a little more than three miles to the falls. I once encountered what I believe was bear scat on the southern edge of the Stewart Ranch Property. Just a few months later, two bear cubs were found without their mother on the eastern slope of the Santa Ana Mountains, less than ten miles south of here.

The Morgan Trail continues to the north of the private ranch and into Round Potrero. This spectacular grassland meadow is an idyllic setting and one of my favorite spots in the Santa Ana Mountains. From Round Potrero, the Morgan Trail continues westward for approximately one more mile to its junction with Bear Canyon Trail. This a great day hike, and with two cars, a party can hike through Bear Canyon Trail to the San Juan parking area. Even out-and-back hikes are worth the trip, as this short and easy hike covers several habitats and experiences.

Horsethief Trail (East and West)

Horsethief Trail is an old trail used by natives for at least five hundred years. It got its name from presumed use by horse thieves stealing horses from the ranchos on both sides of the range. Major Horace Bell chased some of these thieves up and out of Coldwater Canyon on the east side of the range and down this trail into Trabuco Canyon. It has been known as Horsethief Trail ever since. The Horsethief Trail (West) shares some of its distance with the Trabuco Trail and thus shares the same scenery. Spectacular Conifer Forest communities and views from Mexico to Ventura can be had from this trail.

Horsethief East drops down from the Main Divide Road about three-quarters of a mile south of where Horsethief West meets the road. The trail follows the southern ridge of Horsethief Canyon down toward the Alberhill Ranch area of Lake Elsinore. Along its way, the trail cuts through chaparral as it drops steeply to the foot of the mountains below.

Coldwater Trail

At the time of this writing, the Coldwater Trail does not really exist. Well, at least its trailhead doesn't. In 1976, the Emissaries of Divine Light purchased the Glen Ivy Hot Springs property and cut off public access to this trail. As late as 2012, the new managers of the hot springs property have pledged to reopen the trail. In order for this to happen, the first quarter mile will need to be rebuilt.

Once this happens, the trail will follow the south ridge of Coldwater Canyon for nine miles to the Main Divide Road at the saddle between Modjeska and

Santiago Peaks. Views into Coldwater Canyon will be worth the steep climb. This is perhaps the wettest canyon in the range and abounds with lush growth, including grapevines as big as my arms. The chaparral that surrounds the trail is dense, having gone nearly three decades without a major fire. Mountain lions, coyotes and deer currently use the upper reach of trail.

Recently, the Warrior Society Mountain Biking Club has done some trail work on the upper sections of the trail and has stated that it would be willing to work on the lower end as well. In any case, there will need to be arrangements made for parking and access. This will be a great addition to the Santa Ana Mountains trail system when complete.

Bedford Trail

Bedford Truck Trail is just that—a truck trail. Though the U.S. Forest Service keeps the gate closed most of the time and there is little or no parking at the gate, it does represent a major eastern route up the range. Check with the Trabuco Ranger District for access. The route is easy to see and follow, even from the Temescal Valley below, as the forest service used the route to create a major firebreak more than three hundred feet wide. The scar is still visible more than six years after the catastrophe.

Bedford Truck Trail climbs quickly some 2,500 feet up the eastern escarpment and passes through chaparral with little or no shade. What makes this route worth the steep climb are the views. As you climb, more and more of the Inland Empire spreads out below. On clear days, one can see all of the high peaks of the Transverse and Peninsular Ranges. Much of the Santa Ana Mountains' eastern slope can also be seen from this hike. The nearby Bedford Canyon was once home to Nick Earp, father of the famed lawman Wyatt Earp. Today, the canyon is seen by some as the best place to tunnel through the range.

Coal Canyon

Coal Canyon is as important a place as the Santa Ana Mountains have within their shrub-covered ridges and canyons. It is home to rare species such as the northernmost Tecate cypress trees in the world. It is also the preferred path of travel for the mountain lions that utilize both the Santa Ana Mountains and the Chino Hills and points north.

The trail that climbs this canyon is really more of a road than trail, though automobile travel has been prohibited. Today, only foot, horse and bike travel are permitted up and down the trail. Along the way, the trail passes mule fat bottomlands and Coastal Sage Scrub and bits of Chaparral communities. Near the top of Coal Canyon, as well as in Gypsum Canyon to the west, one encounters the only Tecate cypress trees in the United States. Until a recent fire, the oldest and largest Tecate cypress trees in the world grew here. In those trees and the other old-growth specimens that were found nearby lived California spotted owls. Today, one can encounter tiny Tecate cypress seedlings in the drainages that flow from this grove so that this forest will continue to provide a habitat for the rare species of owl found in the Santa Ana Mountains. Although fire destroyed the old trees, it also gave them life, as the hard cones of these trees only open to release their seeds following a hot fire.

Coal Canyon is named for the coal mines that were once worked in the upper reaches of this canyon. Now, the lower canyon is part of Chino Hills State Park so that the wildlife corridor can be maintained between the mountains and the hills. The upper reaches are an ecological reserve set aside to protect the Tecate cypress forest. You can access this canyon from Green River Road and the Santa Ana River.

San Juan Loop and Chiquito Trails

The San Juan Loop and Chiquito Trails are easily accessed off Ortega Highway at the San Juan Loop parking area across from the Ortega Candy Store. This lot is located about eighteen and a half miles from Interstate 5. The San Juan Loop Trail is likely the easiest trail in the Santa Ana Mountains, with less than three miles of total distance and only four hundred feet of elevation change.

Most of the San Juan Loop follows Bear Canyon Creek and is shaded with alder, willow and sycamore trees. The remainder of the trail crosses buckwheat, laurel sumac and other shrubs along a rocky stretch of Long Canyon. This section has little shade, though it is only about a mile in distance.

For those who seek a little more distance, elevation change and variety, jump onto the Chiquito Trail at about the halfway point along the San Juan Loop Trail. The Chiquito Trail follows the ridge above Long Canyon and then cuts across the ridge into Lion Canyon. Here, there are spectacular oaks that shade the trail nearly all the way to the Chiquito Springs Forest. Lion Canyon is named for the big cats that frequent this area.

From this forest, about eight and a half miles from the parking area, the trail climbs up and into Blue Jay Campground. This route is popular with mountain bikers, yet hikers can also enjoy the route, especially if they start at Blue Jay Campground and hike down toward the parking area.

Water and restrooms are available at the parking area, and food, snacks and souvenirs can be purchased at the candy store across Ortega Highway.

Santiago Truck Trail

Santiago Truck Trail is a hot, dry route almost all the way to Santiago Peak. Shade can be found as the trail wraps around small peaks and road cuts that block the sun at certain times during the day. The trail traverses brush and chaparral that include almost-pure stands of Molina or bear grass. Some of these stands became visible only following the Santiago fire of 2007.

Along the Santiago Truck Trail's route are a few historical points of interest. Vulture Crags is a collection of rocky outcroppings that form spires and buttes. This area was once home to many California condors. They nested on these unique geologic features and soared above Santiago Canyon and the Orange County coastal plain during the day.

At the seven-and-a-half-mile mark, the trail is almost level with the creek. Here, travelers find Old Camp. This is an excellent trail camp that has been used for at least 135 years. From here, Joplin Trail continues up to Santiago Peak. The adventurous can turn here and take Santiago Creek back to the parking area, although those who choose this route must realize that this is not a trail route and they are likely to get wet along the way. The creek has water most of the year here, and numerous deep pools provide refreshing swims in the spring and early summer in wet years. Between Old Camp and Bear Trap Canyon, hikers find evidence of early mining attempts. Perhaps these are the unsuccessful silver claims of Tule Woods, who found a little silver in Santiago Canyon prior to the big boom in Silverado. Bear Trap Canyon is a hanging canyon with an impressive little waterfall in early spring (later in wet years).

You can access Santiago Truck Trail off Modjeska Grade Road, which connects Santiago Canyon Road with Modjeska Road. There is little legal parking in this area, as mountain biking is popular here, and there have been some over-parking issues in the past decade. Just follow the direction of posted signs, and you will be okay.

Harding Canyon

Harding Canyon was the first canyon in the Santa Ana Mountains that I really explored. I first ventured up the route to Harding Canyon Falls in 1985 with my close friend Craig Benneville. We both became avid defenders of wilderness and went on to explore the Santa Ana Mountains together for many years. When I moved to the Southwest, he went to the Northwest. I was in Prescott, Arizona, and he was in Eugene, Oregon. Eventually, Craig died, falling from a two-hundred-foot Douglas fir while topping it to create snag habitat. I think of him every time I go to Harding Canyon, though we had adventures in Blackstar, Peters, Trabuco and other points in the Santa Anas as well.

Harding Canyon is accessed from the Harding Truck Trail out of Modjeska Canyon. Park near Tucker Wildlife Sanctuary and follow the truck trail up to the eroded spur road that obviously drops into the next canyon to the north. This is Harding Canyon. The view from this point is extensive, overlooking the sycamore woodlands and a series of braided trails that lead into the dense Riparian tangle of the canyon. Various grottos have been carved from the sedimentary layers across the canyon from the overlook and reportedly were the hideouts of numerous bandits in the past.

Once you drop into the canyon, you have a choice of going downstream to the old dam or upstream some five miles to the falls. This route consists of boulder-hopping, poison oak–dodging, pool-crossing travel. Though it sounds difficult, every turn in the canyon makes it more worthwhile. Steep walls, Humboldt lilies and deep year-round pools that may still contain steelhead trout can be found up the canyon. As for the fish, mudslides following the 2007 fire may have finally pushed them out. I like to believe that the resilience of our native species is greater than we give them credit. In fact, if you had asked the same biologists who declare them gone now if they were there just twenty years ago, they would have told you that no steelhead remain in the range. They have been found in several locations since.

Harding Canyon Falls is a spectacular waterfall, although it is not one of the highest in the range. I once climbed the falls but don't recommend that others follow my stupidity. It is much nicer from the bottom looking up than from the top looking down.

Maple Springs Trail

Maple Springs Truck Trail starts where Silverado Canyon Road ends. There is some parking here, though an Adventure Pass is required. The Maple Springs Visitors' Center is also located here and is staffed by volunteers. This trail continues to follow Silverado Canyon as it climbs more than four thousand feet to Santiago Peak. The distance is about ten miles.

Silverado Canyon was once known as Madera Canyon, which translates to "wood canyon," because the largest stands of Coulter pine can be found here. Much of the area was logged heavily in the 1870s and '80s. The trees of this canyon built the towns of Silverado and Carbondale.

Maple Springs can be found about six miles up from the gate and have been so named because of the big-leaf maples that grow around the springs. In winter, this area often gets snowed on, and the hike up the canyon is always fun. Snow never lasts long in the Santa Ana Mountains, so when it happens, you have to enjoy it quickly.

Main Divide Road (South)

The South Main Divide Road begins at Ortega Highway and continues south to Tenaja Road, although technically this includes Wildomar and Los Alisos Roads. The South Main Divide, according to U.S. Forest Service maps, drops down the east slope to a usually locked gate above the town of

Joel Robinson on the Main Divide Road.

157

Wildomar. The entire South Main Divide Road is chip sealed, making it passenger-vehicle safe.

As the Main Divide Road leaves Ortega Highway, it passes the El Cariso Nature Trail and the Firefighters Memorial Picnic Area. The pine trees in this area are mostly Monterey pines and were planted as part of the Penny Pines Program. In about two miles, the road passes the Morgan trailhead. Then, in two more miles, the road crosses Morrell Potrero and the Rancho Capistrano community. The road makes it to the Wildomar Off-Highway Vehicle Park and Campground in another couple miles. From this point, the South Main Divide travels along a mostly wild and undeveloped landscape to its connection with Tenaja Road and the Tenaja parking area.

Main Divide Road (North)

The North Main Divide Road is more clearly defined than its counterpart to the south. Running between Ortega Highway on the south and Sierra Peak to the north, this forty-mile route along the high ridge of the Santa Ana

Main Divide Road North.

Mountains is like no other journey in the range. The North Main Divide Road makes connection to all of the highest peaks, including both Modjeska and Santiago, the high points of Old Saddleback. This road is literally the spine of the range running its distance, and with places with significant drops on either side of the road, it is not for the inexperienced driver.

In addition to the peaks of the range, the North Main Divide Road makes connection to most of the major trails and canyons of the northern Santa Ana Mountains, providing for a number of long hikes or rides through the range. I have used this road on several occasions to make multiday backpacking trips in the northern Santa Ana Mountains.

Views from the Main Divide Road go in all directions. One can really look over the Santa Ana Mountains along this road. In addition, views into Mexico, Los Angeles and the Channel Islands are no problem on clear days.

There are locked gates at Beeks Place, south of the Main Divide's junction with Black Star Canyon, so permission to pass here is required for larger vehicles. Those on foot, horseback or bike (motorcycle) will have no problem getting by. Portions of the road also get closed during summer and fall, when threat of fire is at its highest.

PART IV

Conservation and the Future

For as much as the twentieth century changed the Santa Ana Mountains, the twenty-first century may make those last one hundred years pale in comparison. In the world of conservation, it is the next one hundred years—or for that matter, the next one hundred days—that are the most important. Sitting in offices somewhere, men are planning roads, towns, tunnels, mines and all of the bells and whistles that go along with them. At the same time, there are people roaming the slopes, canyons and ridges of the Santa Ana Mountains discovering new things and rediscovering old ones. As has been the case many times before, these two groups will eventually run head-on into each other. The outcome of these collisions is the future of the Santa Ana Mountains.

Residential and industrial development is always on the radar of conservation activists, and many projects that would swallow pieces of the Santa Ana Mountains have made it to the drawing board; some have even made it to the chambers of city councils and county supervisors. Larger projects, like those on the Mission Viejo and Irvine Ranches, have been well planned, with all of the parts and pieces looked at closely. That is not to say they are good projects, only that they are meticulously planned. Other projects, such as those by smaller landowners, often make it through the regulatory process with less-intensive review. In many cases, these projects are the ones that block biological corridors, confine streams to channels and destroy natural and historical resources. Activists must diligently watch all proposed development in the Santa Ana Mountains to ensure that only the best planned projects make it onto the ground.

Because most of the land in the Santa Ana Mountains is owned by the federal government and managed by the Cleveland National Forest, much of what happens in the range occurs under their watch. As discussed in previous sections of this book, the Trabuco Ranger District is not a timber-rich place of old-growth forests or geologically cursed with gold veins running deep beneath its ridges. No, the Santa Ana Mountains are just plain old guardians of healthy, wild watersheds. In economic terms, this simply means that there are no revenue-generating resources in the Trabuco Ranger District that make this place important politically. Hence, the budgets allotted for the Trabuco are smaller than required to adequately provide for the many needs of the forest.

In addition to small budgets, the lack of revenue generation has made the Trabuco Ranger District a stepping stone for many district rangers who either sharpen their teeth here before moving on to more prestigious positions in forests with trees or minerals or use the Trabuco as a last step before retirement. Together, these conditions have at times taken their toll on the range. This does not mean that the rangers of the Trabuco are bad people or that they do not care about the Santa Ana Mountains. They are dedicated to their jobs and on almost all accounts are good at what they do. As a writer and naturalist, I have the luxury of looking in on a situation with no personal consequences to my analysis. The good people in the U.S. Forest Service do not have this luxury. I do often disagree with their decisions and their management styles, but I do not fault them for it. I have worked closely with many forest service representatives over the last twenty-five years and have learned much from all of them. This book would not be possible were it not for the assistance and shared resources of the Trabuco Ranger District.

That said, many of the challenges of the twenty-first century will rest in the offices of the Trabuco Ranger District or at its parent site, the Cleveland National Forest headquarters in San Diego County. Some of these challenges are discussed below; others are yet to be discovered.

Off-road vehicles are one of the scourges of the range. There are many responsible operators of fun, exciting and powerful off-road vehicles; unfortunately, most of them choose to operate their machines somewhere else. For decades, the Santa Ana Mountains have been crisscrossed with illegal trails and roads that cause unmeasured disturbance to waterways through erosion and sedimentation. Following rain, teenagers, both by actual age or just by mentality, tear through the range, throwing mud on themselves and one another while cutting scars through habitats that will take a century to heal. Although many of those scars are still visible today, the U.S. Forest Service has beefed up its enforcement efforts in the last ten years, and that increase has shown positive effects on the range and lessened the damage of illegal off-roaders. The forest service has also increased its work with volunteers who have restored many old roads and other scars of misuse. I have worked with groups like the Peninsular Ranges Biodiversity Project to close and restore several illegal roads in the Tenaja Area of the range. The Forest District has a transportation plan that calls out the actual mileage of roads it will allow and manage and how many miles it will close, open or restore in a given period of time. It's up to the public, for whom this land is managed, to make sure they are following the plan.

Activities like off-road vehicles have also caused an increase in invasive pest plants. Many of these plants invade disturbed areas such as old roads' track scars. In other cases, new roads and road-repair projects have been the source of these invaders.

Plants such as Mediterranean fountain grass were introduced on purpose as erosion-control efforts along road cuts. *Arondo donax*, also known as giant cane, was introduced to stabilize stream banks and now has taken over stretches of many waterways in and around the range. These plants have little habitat value as they do not provide food or shelter for wildlife, and they tend to choke out the plants that do provide these functions. Control and removal of invasive plants is an important management task that in most cases will also fall on the public to enforce and carry out.

Invasive species often increase fire dangers as well. The Trabuco Ranger District takes its fire prevention and protection seriously, as is made evident by the recent efforts to make firebreaks three hundred feet wide. Travel anywhere in the Inland Empire of Southern California and these scars can be seen running up the ridgeline slopes of the Santa Anas like bad tattoos. I understand the need for fire protection efforts; however, taking such an industrial approach discounts other values the mountains deliver. These include habitat, view sheds and more. When the land managers treat the forest this way, so then do the users of the range. I was once told by a National Park firefighter in Yellowstone National Park that during the firestorm of 1988, the only firebreak that worked was Yellowstone Lake, which was ten miles wide. When a fire is fueled by seventy-mile-an-hour Santa Ana Winds, a three-hundred-foot firebreak stops nothing. I urge the forest service to seek alternatives to this practice.

Other threats to the Santa Ana Mountains are more sinister. The LEAPS project is one example of this. LEAPS stands for the Lake Elsinore Advanced Pump Storage Project, which is a fancy name for a proposed hydroelectric-generation project. This in and of itself is not bad; however, the process and impacts on the Santa Ana Mountains would be significant and destructive.

First envisioned by the Elsinore Valley Municipal Water District in 1988, the LEAPS project is now being pushed by the water district's contractor, Nevada Hydro, which did not form until 1997 and has no other projects outside of the LEAPS project.

First, a 180-foot-high dam has been proposed for Morrell Canyon. This dam would be visible from the Morgan Trail within the San Mateo Canyon Wilderness and from Ortega Highway. The related reservoir would flood more than one hundred acres of old-growth oak woodlands in Morrell Canyon, destroy sacred sites for the Luiseno and Juaneño tribal groups and cause irreparable damage to the quality of the San Mateo Canyon Wilderness area.

The LEAPS project, as it's proposed, would pump water out of Lake Elsinore and up to the reservoir during low electrical demand periods, when electrical rates are lower, and then release the water back into Lake Elsinore during peak demand periods, generating electricity at a profit. A massive system of transmission lines would be required to connect and receive electricity from the existing grid system. Mores than thirty miles of high-voltage transmission lines would run from Escondido to Corona. All of these elements raise flags for defenders of the Santa Ana Mountains. There is the loss of habitat, destruction of viewscapes and increased fire danger. Hang gliding enthusiasts have also raised concerns that the transmission lines pose dangers to their participants and would essentially eliminate their ability to use the Elsinore Peak and ridge area for gliding.

The risks of LEAPS far outweigh the benefits here, and it is my opinion that for the benefit of the Santa Ana Mountains, the project should be eliminated from the planning boards.

Other projects that impact the Santa Ana Mountains and continue to come and go and come again include a tunnel through the range. Although at the time of pounding out these words, no current proposal is officially being discussed, the idea of a tunnel through the Santa Ana Mountains just will not go away.

There have been discussions of tunnels to deliver water, tunnels for trains and tunnels for roads. The latter seems to gain the most momentum, though it has never made it past a draft environmental review. What most concerns me is that the proposed tunnels' path—Bedford Canyon to the Ladd or Silverado areas—has not been preserved or protected and thus will continue to be viewed as a viable option. Geologic tests have been conducted and determined that the mountains' water table would be altered. In addition, the Santa Ana Mountains are the offspring of earthquakes; thus, any tunnel would be susceptible to the many faults of the area.

The most recent incarnation of the tunnel was an extension of the Mid County Parkway, a road that would connect the town of San Jacinto to Interstates 215 and 15. If approved, the road would follow Cajalco Road from the 215 to the 15 and then follow Bedford Canyon through the mountains, depositing drivers onto Santiago Canyon Road in Orange County. The alterations and infrastructure this would cause on both side of the Santa Anas would forever destroy the rural setting. All one must do is look to Orange County's toll roads to see the damage that would be caused.

It is not too late to stop the tragedies discussed here. In fact, there is an effort underway that would put a stop to the destructive practices, poorly planned projects and bad ideas. It would do so while increasing recreational opportunities, improving economic conditions in the small communities within the range and giving the larger cities that border the range a reason to connect with and preserve the Santa Ana Mountains. This effort is known as the Grizzly Bear National Monument.

Put forth by the Santa Ana Mountains Wild Heritage Project and the California Chaparral Institute, the Grizzly Bear National Monument (GBNM) would convert the Trabuco Ranger District from a Department of Agriculture and U.S. Forest Service property to one of the Department of Interior and the National Park Service. The change in management priorities would instantly improve the ecological balance within the mountains by taking a more holistic approach to the range instead of the purely utilitarian approach instituted now. The effort to create the Grizzly Bear National Monument is supported by more than one hundred organizations, businesses and individuals.

Creation of the GBNM would create economic incentives to preserve and promote the range. Rural canyon communities would now be seen as gateways to the park, and the preservation of these rural settings would be in the economic interest of the communities. A rural transportation system could accompany the designation, creating jobs for tram drivers and tour guides. New retail stores, hotels and restaurants would be developed in Corona, Lake Elsinore, San Juan Capistrano and Orange. Quaint boutiques selling the products of local artists would spring up in Silverado and El Cariso Village. Tour companies would lead mountain bike and horseback rides, and backpacking trips would give local students new employment opportunities.

Projects like LEAPS and proposals for tunnels would now be forced to meet a new level of approvals and face tougher scrutiny. But most of all, the Grizzly Bear National Monument would give the Santa Ana Mountains the protection and prominence they deserve and preserve for countless generations to come the opportunity to see, experience and learn from them.

Resources

Government Agencies

Federal

Trabuco Ranger District, Cleveland National Forest
1147 East Sixth Street
Corona, CA 92879
(951) 736-1811

U.S. Fish and Wildlife Service
6010 Hidden Valley Road
Carlsbad, CA 92011
(760) 431-9440
www.fws.gov

State

California Department of Fish and Game
4949 Viewridge Avenue
San Diego, CA 92123
(858) 467-4201
www.dfg.ca.gov

CALIFORNIA DEPARTMENT OF PARKS AND RECREATION
Inland Empire District
17801 Lake Perris Drive
Perris, CA 92571
(951) 443-2423

County

ORANGE COUNTY HARBORS, BEACHES AND PARKS
1 Irvine Park Road
Orange, CA 92869
(714) 973-6865
www.ocparks.com

RIVERSIDE COUNTY OPEN SPACE AND PARKS DISTRICT
4600 Crestmore Road
Riverside, CA 92509
(951) 955-4310
www.riversidecountyparks.org

NONPROFIT ORGANIZATIONS

INLAND EMPIRE WATERKEEPER
6876 Indiana Avenue, Suite D
Riverside, CA 92506
(951) 530-8823
www.iewaterkeeper.org

IRVINE RANCH CONSERVANCY
4727 Portola Parkway
Irvine, CA 92620
(714) 508-4757

NATURALIST FOR YOU
Post Office Box 381
Silverado, CA 92676
(714) 649-9084
naturalist-for-you.org

RANCHO DE ORTEGA LEARNING RANCH
411 Seventh Street
Norco, CA 92860
(951)258-0017
www.rdolearningranch.webs.com

SANTA ANA MOUNTAINS WILD HERITAGE PROJECT
www.santaanamountains.org

TRAIL4ALL
13720 Florine Avenue
Paramount, CA 90723
(310) 344-9229
Trails4All.org

THE WILDLANDS CONSERVANCY
39611 Oak Glen Road #12
Oak Glen, CA 92399
(909) 797-8507
www.wildlandsconservancy.org

About the Author

Patrick Mitchell is the director of natural history and agricultural programs for the Heritage Museum of Orange County in Santa Ana, California. He is the author of *Santa Ana River Guide: From Crest to Coast*. He has been a ranch manager, resort landscapes director, park naturalist, herb farmer, environmental activist and field ecologist.